Take the Crown!

18 Core Principles to Grow Your Business and Improve Your Life

Praise for TAKE THE CROWN!

Miles Schnaer has an unwavering commitment — to his faith, to his family, to his business. He always strives to do the right thing. There may be bumps along the way, but he embraces, and even relishes, the challenges. Miles has worked hard to get where he is, but he's acutely aware that he didn't do it alone. His adherence to the principles in this book has helped inspire those around him to achievements they likely didn't realize they were capable of.

> — **Kendall Gammon,** Author, Speaker, and
> 15-year NFL Veteran

Miles Schnaer's formula for success in his business and personal life is something we can all learn from.

> — **Bill Self,** University of Kansas Head Basketball
> Coach and Member of the Naismith Memorial
> Basketball Hall of Fame

Miles Schnaer understands that the auto industry is all about people and products. His business philosophy is all about having the right team, the right products, and putting the customers first. He has stayed true to these core values and, as a result, his is a success story that we can all learn from.

> — **Bob Carter,** Executive Vice President, Toyota
> Motors North America

Miles Schnaer has set the standard, not only with his excellent customer service but also through his generous civic endeavors. As you read this book, you'll understand that he is very mindful of the way he lives his life and believes that when you conduct yourself the right way good things will happen to you.

— **Sharon Spratt,** Chief Executive Officer, Cottonwood, Inc.

Miles has been recognized by his peers for his entrepreneurial skills. His dedication to his family and his consistency in setting the right example have been the pillars of Miles' success, as you'll understand after reading his story.

— **Larry Van Tuyl,** CEO, Van Tuyl Companies

As a businessman, Miles Schnaer has navigated the ups and downs of the automotive world. By knowing how to recruit, retain, and assess talent, he leads from a set of principles and ideals that are reflected in all his decisions. As you'll read, he is obsessed with treating people right. His generosity in his business dealings is as conspicuous as it is in his community and philanthropic endeavors. While understanding his heart is essential in comprehending his story, it is his business acumen and insights that make him a success. His motto is "Make great things happen." That is his advice for everyone he meets.

— **Dr. Steve Scott,** President, Pittsburg State University

As a dealer with very high market share and customer experience scores, Miles' success speaks for itself. What is most impressive about Miles is the way he goes about achieving this success. He is a complete gentleman to work with, his word can be completely trusted, and it is important to him to conduct business the right way.

— **Scott Bell,** Central Region Vice President,
Volkswagen Group of America

Miles and my dad Max were great friends for many years, enjoying laughs, lunch, and KU sports. Everyone should be so lucky to have a friend like Miles Schnaer, who provides sound and sage advice on life and business. His practices and principles are applicable across a wide spectrum.

— **Kurt Falkenstien**

It is rare to find a person that possesses the strong business acumen and personal compassion for others that Miles lives on a daily basis. His sincerity and philosophy jump off the pages. He doesn't just talk the talk, he truly walks the walk of a true leader.

— **Sheahon Zenger,** Director of Athletics and
Recreation, University of New Haven

Miles Schnaer truly exemplifies what is right about the retail automotive industry. Having always exhibited exceptional performance in his dealerships, his distinguished community service has impacted and benefitted thousands of lives over his career. While Miles has left no stone unturned in his business life, he holds his faith and family paramount to his success.

— **Don McNeely,** President, Kansas Automobile
Dealers Association

Take the Crown!

18 Core Principles to Grow Your Business and Improve Your Life

Miles Schnaer

with Mark Fitzpatrick

Requests for permission should be addressed to: Ascend Books, LLC, Attn: Rights and Permissions Department, 11722 West 91st Street, Overland Park, KS 66214

First Edition
10 9 8 7 6 5 4 3 2 1
ISBN: print book 978-1-7369431-9-9
Ebook ISBN: 978-1-7369431-5-1
Library of Congress Control Number:2022932335

Publisher: Bob Snodgrass
Editor: Courtney Brown
Publication Coordinator: Molly Gore
Sales and Marketing: Lenny Cohen
Dust Jacket and Book Design: Rob Peters

All photos courtesy of Miles Scanner unless otherwise indicated.

Publisher's Note: The goal of Ascend Books is to publish quality works. With that goal in mind, we are proud to offer this book to our readers. Please notify the publisher of any erroneous credits or omissions, and corrections will be made to subsequent editions/future printings. Please note, however, that the story, experiences, and the words are those of the authors alone.

All names, logos, and symbols that appear in this book are trademarks of their individual organizations and institutions. This notice is for the protection of trademark rights only, and in no way represents the approval or disapproval of the text or photos of this book by those organizations or institutions.

Printed in Canada

www.ascendbooks.com

Contents

Dedication

To Paula, Mandi, Ali, and Maddox

FOREWORD

There are many examples of people who have been successful in business, or in their personal lives, or in philanthropy, or in service, but few achieve success across all aspects of the human experience. Miles Schnaer is one of those rare individuals who has done exactly that. And because of that, there is much to learn from his experiences and his story.

My connection to Miles has been through my work at Pittsburg State University. Not long after I took on the role of President, we began to see each other on a regular basis at university events. His ties to the university are deep, given that he earned his bachelor's degree from Pitt State in 1971. More importantly, he met his wife, Paula, on our campus. While he had always been proud of his alma mater, in recent years his connections to the university have been renewed.

Having led Pittsburg State now for more than a decade and served the campus in a variety of leadership roles, along with community and national leadership positions, I have developed a sense of what it takes to be a leader and to be successful in life. As I think about Miles and the way he conducts himself as a husband, father, grandfather, businessman, philanthropist, and man of faith, I see a person who has mastered life, but who possesses such genuine humility that he'll never think of himself that way.

As a businessman he has navigated the ups and downs of the automotive world to build multiple successful dealerships. By knowing how to recruit, retain, and assess the right talent, he leads from a set of principles and ideals that he can clearly articulate, and they are reflected in all of his decisions. As you'll see, he is obsessed with treating people right, and when it comes to his customers, they are always on the winning side of any transaction with him. He has a heart that is as evident in his business dealings as it is in his community and philanthropic endeavors. While understanding his heart is valuable, it is his business acumen and insights that are applicable to every sector of the economy, and not just the car business. You'll quickly see how true that is.

Pittsburg State University looks and feels different because of the investments Miles and Paula have made over the years. His engagement in our foundation as a member of the Board of Trustees, as well as on the Executive Committee, was exemplary, always imploring us to pursue excellence. And, as donors, he and Paula were ready to step forward with the financial commitments to make great things happen. In that work, I will always see him as a valued partner and colleague.

Although Miles' contributions at my institution have been quite significant, they do not fully reflect his record of philanthropy. His heart is in helping those within our communities who are less fortunate, particularly those with disabilities. His support has made a difference in the lives of countless individuals who often get overlooked. But not by Miles; he sees them, recognizes their needs, and sets about to help them.

And then, of course, there is his family. Miles is the consummate family man. He is so devoted to Paula, his two daughters, and his grandson. They truly are the joys of his life. I've always thought that people who have great families make great friends. And that's true with Miles. He knows the meaning of friendship as a giver, a supporter, a listener, and an encourager. I've been on the receiving side of this from Miles, and, like he's done for so many others, he has enriched my life with our friendship.

Finally, Miles is a man of deep faith and a commitment to that faith. This shows in his treatment of others, his compassion for those less fortunate, and his hope for better days ahead. His spirit brings joy and optimism to those with whom he interacts. His overt compassion and sensitivity to others provide a model for others to follow. And he demonstrates that these characteristics can be present in a business, enabling that business to thrive and be sustainable over time.

As his friend, I cannot imagine Miles honoring me in a more profound way than to ask me to pen the foreword to his book. I trust you'll enjoy reading Miles' thoughts about his work and his life. He's been successful in both, and, because of that, I know his principles will bring value to you, to those you work with, and to those you love.

Steve Scott
President, Pittsburg State University

INTRODUCTION

As I completed my biology exam in 1971 at Pittsburg State University, I knew it hadn't gone well.

I had served in the pathology labs while in the service during the Vietnam era, and after I left the Army my dream was to attend medical school and study pathology. But with the normal distractions of college life in the 1970s I had trouble focusing on academics, and the results bordered on mediocrity. The dream was quickly fading.

This test might as well have been written in a foreign language, and I had little optimism that I had done enough to get the grade I would need to pass the course. The professor was Dr. Keller, a no-nonsense academic with little patience for those who underperformed. I walked up to him after the exam and told him that I knew I'd done poorly, but I needed a D in the class to graduate. He said, "Come see me in the morning."

I couldn't sleep that night. When I went into his office his first statement was direct.

"You're right. You flunked the test."

My knees got weak and my stomach churned, but I mustered enough gumption to say, "If you'll give me a D for the course, I can graduate. If you don't, I'll have to come back and take this class again next year."

Apparently, the thought of that was as repugnant to him as it was terrifying to me, because after a long pause he looked at me and said, "I'll pass you, but you have to promise you'll never go to any type of medical school."

I agreed immediately — I'd just negotiated my first successful deal! Not long afterward, I was bound for the auto sales business.

I suppose I owe a great deal to Dr. Keller, because overall it's been a heck of a ride ever since. I've had a great career that's been financially and spiritually rewarding. My dedication to some basic values I was taught in my youth, along with some others I've learned along the way has brought me success far beyond what I could ever have imagined as that distracted, party-going college student of a half century ago.

And while the material benefits have been great, the greatest reward is the feeling that I may have helped improve life for those around me — for my wife, daughters, and grandson; for my business associates and employees; for the leaders and citizens of the communities in which I have lived and worked; and maybe even for a few folks with whom I've had chance encounters along the way. I've been granted many blessings, and there's nothing I enjoy more than sharing them. I'm proud that I've been able to give back, both to the community and to those who have aided me on my life's journey.

From those relationships came the inspiration to write this book. It is my desire that readers of these pages can be guided by some of the same beliefs and strategies that I have. I hope your goal is to go out and make other lives better, and for those lives to then do the same. I've always been a fan of the multiplier effect.

I've achieved far more than I could have ever expected as a middling student from a Midwestern, working-class Jewish family. The fates have been benevolent to me, but I've also worked hard — sometimes too hard — and taken some chances. I found a career I enjoyed, and I pursued it with passion. I had great mentors and associates, and I learned to believe in myself and what I could accomplish.

And the foundation for that began, as it often does, long before I arrived on the scene. It's because of the determination of my parents and my immigrant grandparents to make good in the face of discrimination and hardship that I enjoyed a positive and supportive upbringing and a successful and productive life.

I've often wished that my parents had shared more about their own formative years, more of the tenets that they used to shape their lives and inspire them to be solid citizens and model parents. I wish I knew more about how they got where they did. Their lives were compelling, and, though all I have is their oral history, I'm proud to include some of it here as part of my own.

Through the years I've built upon the foundation they gave me and acquired a set of principles to which I've faithfully adhered. There are 18 — coincidentally a significant number in the Jewish faith. If you've ever celebrated a toast with a Jewish friend ("L'chaim!"), you might know that the word "chai" in Hebrew means "life" and represents the idea of being alive. Each letter in the Hebrew alphabet represents a number, and "chai" is spelled using the letters "het" and "yud," which are the equivalents of eight and 10 respectively. This adds up to 18 and has made that number synonymous with the word. I didn't magically pick the number, nor did I shoot for it just so that it would be in concert with my faith, but it feels right that it worked out that way.

This is my opportunity to share those principles, which are applicable to nearly anyone in any type of position. Whether you own a business, work in the private or public sector, are active in a not-for-profit or charitable organization, or just want to lay the foundation for a better life, these fundamental concepts can be of benefit. They can fuel the determination to succeed, but also provide perspective and insight into maintaining a healthy balance between our professional and personal lives, which was, unfortunately, not something I truly realized early in my own career.

I have made plenty of mistakes along the way, and you'll see clearly that it took me a while to find my place in life and determine where I wanted to go, both as a person and as a businessman. There were struggles and challenges, but I had a lot of help and guidance from some pretty special people, both in and outside of my family, and I trust my mistakes will hold as many lessons as my successes.

My experiences have left me in a pretty good place today, but not completely satisfied with what I'll leave behind. I'm a storyteller, and I like to think I have some good ones to share. But while much of my personal history is included here, this is not a biography. Rather, it is my hope that these stories will help show the practical application and value of the principles that have guided me.

I've had a great journey, and I never would have gotten to this point without the support of many family members and friends, but I needed structure to go to the next level. These 18 core principles have provided that structure, and I hope that you will enjoy learning about them as much as I have experienced a rewarding life because of them.

Chapter 1
BE INSPIRED

Principle #1: Learn from those who've gone before so you can pass it on.

"What to do with a mistake: recognize it, admit it, learn from it, forget it."
Dean Smith

In the last part of the 19th century, it is estimated that 1.5 million Jews immigrated to the United States from Eastern Europe and Russia, primarily because of political and religious discrimination. That's really where my story begins.

My father's family had its roots in Latvia, which in the 19th century was part of the Russian Empire. In the middle of that century, Latvia had a thriving Jewish community that contributed greatly to the development of industry and trade. However, after the assassination of Czar Alexander II in March 1881, Jews were wrongly blamed for the crime and a wave of anti-Semitism grew in the Russian Empire. Under the rule of the Czar's son and successor, Alexander III, repressive policies and attitudes toward Jews intensified throughout the Empire, which triggered a series of anti-Jewish riots, known as pogroms.

My great-grandfather, Simcha Sorokin, was a rabbi in the city of Rēzekne. He had five children, one of whom, Jankel, died during a pogrom in 1905. The other four managed to escape the country, including two who found their way to New York City. It was there that daughter Hannah met and married Morris Schnaer and gave birth to my father, Abraham Isadore Schnaer, on July 27, 1909.

Dad grew up in Brooklyn with two younger siblings and attended the Columbia University College of Pharmaceutical Sciences after high school. He was a boxer, and though he didn't discuss his pugilistic past much, I know he earned enough as a fighter to largely cover the cost of his education at that prestigious institution.

My mother's family was from Warsaw, Poland, which was also under Russian control in the late 19th century. Even though there was a flourishing Jewish community in Warsaw, there had been growing anti-Semitism and pogroms there as well.

My grandfather, Jacob Greenstein, and grandmother, Fannie Wax, were both born in Warsaw, but, facing continued discrimination, their families moved to the United States around the turn of the century, when they were both teenagers. Though the two families were from the same section of Warsaw, they did not become acquainted until they all happened to end up in Denver. There Jacob and Fannie were married, and their third child, my mother Sylvia, was born on December 28, 1910 — the fourth light of Hanukkah.

Grandpa J.J. Greenstein was a haberdasher, and his business regularly relocated him around the country. When Mom was a young child the family moved to Kansas City, and that's where she grew up. Shortly after she graduated from high school, Grandpa's business took the family to New York, where Mom worked as a stenographer and a secretary. It was there that she met Abraham Schnaer.

My parents connected through the Jewish community in Brooklyn. He was originally interested in my Aunt Ethel before noticing Mom. It certainly led to some awkward family moments at the time, but then Ethel met and fell in love with a guy named Maurice Goodman. The two couples had a double wedding on September 22, 1935.

Mom's family wanted to move back to Kansas City, so after Dad graduated from Columbia the whole clan returned in 1937, where they would settle for the rest of their lives. My parents had two daughters — Bonnie in 1940 and Madeline in 1942 — and then I came along on September 2, 1946.

This family heritage was the backdrop of my development. Despite generations of living with memories of discrimination and persecution, my parents still managed to raise me to have a conscience. Their experiences made them compassionate, and I learned to look at people for who they were rather than what they were. This mindset would always be the backbone of my efforts in business, community work, and, most importantly, my relationships. My hope has been to make a difference in the lives of as many people as I could — regardless of their background, faith, skin tone, or physical limitations.

When I was growing up, our home was comfortable but quite cozy with the five of us, Mom's parents, and her sister Mary all living under the same roof. Grandpa J.J. was even my roommate for a while. Grandma's failing health put Mom in the role of caregiver, a role I never heard her complain about, though it must have been difficult. Our home also became a refuge when relatives passed through Kansas City and needed a temporary (or sometimes more permanent) place to call home. There were also neighborhood kids, friends who came home with me from college, and fellow members of the synagogue who were always in and out of the house. Mom could make anyone feel welcome. Her magnetic personality made it easy to be comfortable in our home and she viewed being hospitable not just as a good thing to do, but the right thing to do. She believed — and taught me — that if you did the right thing in life, you would reap the benefits many times over.

Including his time in New York, Dad was a pharmacist for 44 years. He mainly worked at the West Side Drug Store in downtown Kansas City. It was owned by the Freidsen family, but Dad basically ran it for them as their general manager. He was a loyal employee and very good at his job. We didn't own a car, so Dad took the trolley every day to work. Mom, my sisters, and I would sometimes ride the trolley and meet him for dinner at a Chinese restaurant near the pharmacy. After several mergers and company sales, he ended up with Parkview Drug, from which he eventually retired.

While he was working, Dad would go in early and come home late — a practice that I have adopted myself and promoted to others throughout my career. Dad worked very hard, as did Grandpa J.J., the haberdasher. I didn't really understand it at the time, but as I got older, I came to appreciate their work ethic.

My two sisters were old enough that I know they found me annoying, but they looked out for their little brother and, being good students themselves, were there to help Mom prod me along during my early school days. Bonnie moved out, though, when I was still in elementary school, married an Army ROTC member at the University of Kansas and became a military wife. She was out of the house for good before I turned 14, but Madeline was like a second mother to me as I was growing up. She really provided a lot of guidance and was a big influence on me during my developmental years. Bonnie had a great life and raised a wonderful family with a son and a daughter, but unfortunately passed away from pancreatic cancer in 2018. Madeline is still in the Kansas City area. She married into a family that owned a very successful printing company, and she raised three sons with her husband. She and I remain close although she is now dealing with some health issues.

Growing up, I was pretty much the only Jewish kid in a largely Catholic neighborhood, but I made friends easily, so I always felt right at home and had few issues fitting in. I even occasionally went to midnight Mass with my Catholic friends. I didn't participate but I wanted to learn about their faith. The priest knew me from the neighborhood and didn't mind at all that I attended.

My parents made sure I attended synagogue and Hebrew classes, and I embraced my faith and the activities associated with the Jewish community in Kansas City. They were very religious. They would walk blocks to attend services at their synagogue, while I attended a different one because it had a Hebrew school. Theirs was more orthodox and stricter than the one I attended, but I benefited by having exposure to the different sects of the faith. My parents were extremely active in leadership roles at their synagogue, and their example inspired me to do the same later on whenever I got involved with a community or charitable organization. Mom was especially good about motivating me to attend Hebrew school and becoming a member of the Synagogue Youth Organization, whose conventions I regularly attended. In fact, in 1964 I was named the Kehilath Israel Synagogue Youth of the Year, which was a big honor.

My parents taught me that the reason we are on this earth is to serve and respect others, and this is the cornerstone of my faith and my belief in God. Mom and Dad always set an excellent example for us three children on how to treat people. Thanks to my folks, I learned the true values of life at an early age, and these helped establish in me the principles by which I would later live and do business. Growing up in a Jewish home, we were taught first and foremost about how God created people to have a conscience. As I grew and learned about my heritage, I could trace this ideology as it was passed down through the generations, from my great-grandfather the rabbi to his descendants who eventually found a home in the States.

Dad was a man of high integrity, but on the outside a pretty stoic and tough guy. When my sister Bonnie was in high school, she had a gym teacher who gave her a Persian cat. She brought it home and named it Gym in honor of her instructor. It became ill, and one night we found it dead in the basement. By the time we found the cat, rigor mortis had set in. While my sisters were crying, Dad looked at the corpse, queried "Dead cat?" then grabbed it by the tail and threw it into the garbage can we kept outside by the basement door, without preamble or sentiment.

Dad was also one of those guys who could give you The Look, and you immediately knew you had done something wrong. He was never physical, and I don't recall ever being grounded. The feeling of guilt that resulted from The Look was enough. He knew it was sufficient and used it to great effect. But inside that hard exterior was a heart full of emotion. For instance, whenever Dad talked about the importance of family, he would just start tearing up. I still remember at my wedding when he got up to give a toast. Knowing Dad, none of us knew quite what to expect. But sure enough, not long after he began, he got choked up and had to stop talking for a moment until he could gather himself and continue. I've always been that way, too.

Mom, on the other hand, was our comforter, sounding board, and advisor. She always pushed us to be better, while also providing the support for us to become so. She was always involved at our schools and was a leader for the Girl Scouts and Cub Scouts. She made sure the girls had dance and piano lessons, and that I took music lessons and participated in sports. And friends were always made welcome in our home. One of her best pieces of advice, which she said often, was, "If you expect to get better at what you do, then you need to work at it." Those words have stuck with me through many times of difficulty and weariness.

As for some of life's other lessons, I had the benefit of good neighbors and friends. In junior high school I met Larry Spitcaufsky, who became my best buddy. From Larry I learned to ride horses. On more than one occasion, when we were done riding, he'd push me into a lake or pond, resulting in trouble with my folks when I came home dirty. As has been the way for many mischievous boys, my parents would blame me for causing a stir, and Larry's parents blamed him.

On many weekends we would drive around to barrel racing competitions — Larry was a champion barrel racer — pulling a horse trailer that doubled as our sleeping quarters for the night. It was rough and exhausting, but neither of us would have traded those moments for anything. I still wouldn't.

Larry and his family lived in a brand-new housing development in the south part of Kansas City, across the street from two members of a prominent family whose houses were actually connected by an underground tunnel. I remember many dinners with the Spitcaufsky clan at the Golden Ox

Restaurant in the Kansas City stockyards, where I met all kinds of interesting and unexpected people.

Larry's father was like a second dad to me. When I was in high school, maybe 16 or 17 years old, I "ran away" from home and lived with their family for a couple of days. For years I haven't been able to remember what caused my decampment, but it could have been anything. I wasn't the most calm and thoughtful teenager. Mr. Spitcaufsky eventually talked me into calling my folks and heading back home, but I knew I always had a ready welcome and was cared for there as a sort of extended family member.

I was an outgoing kid which helped me make friends, not just in my Catholic neighborhood and at the Jewish Community center, but also among the kids my age attending the other public and private high schools nearby. Though these friends didn't always like each other, I wended my way through the very different groups. Coming of age in the 1960s, I count my acceptance by such a diverse group of friends as formative. My parents took the time to teach me the principle of respecting others for the simple fact of being human, and my teenage years taught me to practice it.

When I was 16, I had a job with Katz Drug Stores in their record department distribution center downtown. My boss was a guy named Felix Hill, a tall Black man who played part-time in a band. He treated me great and liked to talk about his music. Felix was always looking for new fans and wanted me to get some friends together to come see him play, so I got a group of four together and we drove down one night to see him perform.

When we walked into the bar where his band was playing, I immediately saw Felix on the stage at the far end of the room and started yelling and waving at him. The music stopped and the place went silent. It was then that I realized my friends and

I were the only white faces in the place. It was one of those awkward pin-drop moments that could have been lifted from a movie script. Then Felix saw me and hollered, "Hey, Miles — come on up here!" Chatter resumed, the music restarted, and we received several friendly slaps on the back as we made our way closer to the band. Maybe I was naïve, but it hadn't occurred to me to be cautious about where we were going or what kind of reception we'd receive in any place Felix would be performing. I just wanted to see my friend play.

While most of my early years were uncommonly diverse and accepting, I couldn't escape every consequence of being different myself. I enjoyed sports and did well in the leagues at the Jewish Community Center, but I didn't get the same chance when I attended Southwest High School. I think I could have played basketball, but the coach somehow never managed to find any Jewish students who were good enough for the team — quite a trick since probably 30 percent of the students at the school were Jewish. I knew from my freshman year on that I wouldn't have a chance, so I continued competing at the JCC.

I sang in the choir and was a pretty good musician, but I was not a standout in the classroom. You might assume, given my eventual career in business, that I would have done well with numbers and math, but that was not the case. I didn't necessarily struggle — I just didn't care. I was more interested in hanging out with my friends and participating in my various youth group activities. Even then it was the relationships that held my attention.

My dad didn't act like he cared much about my lack of academic prowess, but, like many Jewish mothers, Mom wanted her son to be a doctor, and I always seemed to be in trouble with her over my schoolwork. My senior year I had a particularly horrific grade on my report card. On my way home, as it burned a hole in my backpack, I stopped at a friend's house and tried to smudge and change it, with the idea that it had "fallen in a puddle." It was an amateurish attempt, and it looked awful, but I was afraid my parents wouldn't let me graduate if I didn't pass the class. Mom, clearly having learned a few things from Dad over the years about how to give The Look, let me twist in silent agony, wondering what academic and personal consequences would befall me. I think she was as aggravated with me over the poor attempt at deception as she was about the abysmal grade. In the end, I graduated, and that's the best I can say about that.

In the fall of 1964, I started at the Metropolitan Community College in Kansas City. My attitude toward academics hadn't changed, but now girls, rather than sports and friends, were my primary distraction. Larry Spitcaufsky had a Corvette, and nearly every Friday at noon we'd jump in it and make the two-hour drive to Columbia, the home of both the University of Missouri and, more appealingly, Stephens College, a private women's college not far from the MU campus.

Unsurprisingly, my freshman year was not an academic success.

With my musical background I did get an A in a music class, but the rest were Cs and Fs — not good enough to keep me in school. Though I had tried futilely to cram for finals and took NoDoz night after night to help me stay awake to study, it made no difference. Adding injury to insult, I wore myself down so far that I spent the following summer sick with mononucleosis and hepatitis. My sisters had gone, so I was now living at home alone with my parents amid frequent visits from Mom's three siblings, none of whom were shy about noting that it didn't appear that I was off and running to a successful career.

Mom's brother, my Uncle Sam, owned a children's clothing company with a plant in Parsons, Kansas, about 150 miles southwest of Kansas City. One day late that summer he came over to our house and said, "What is Miles going to do? He's flunked out of JC and doesn't have a job." He then "offered" to drive me down to Parsons, where there was also a junior college. "You can go to school there and work for me," he declared.

I had no better plan, so we took off to Parsons, and Uncle Sam took me to the junior college to meet the dean, who was an acquaintance. I went through the whole pitiful tale of my flunking out of Metro JC and lacking the grades to initiate a transfer. The dean was an old gentleman who listened patiently to my story, and then said, "I can make it so that you can get into school here."

My uncle looked at me and asked, "What do you want to do?"

Of course, I was all in — I was ready for a fresh start. The dean told me to return home to collect my belongings and come back on Sunday ready to start school the following day.

Uncle Sam and I left and visited a boarding house where he knew they took in students. They had an available room that appeared to be roughly the size of my parents' dining room table.

"I'll take it."

From there we walked across the street to my uncle's plant (it was a very small town), where he had planned for me to work. That was the day I discovered I was allergic to formaldehyde. The instant I walked inside my eyes started burning. Since formaldehyde was used to prevent mildew and wrinkles in the clothes during transportation from the facility, we both knew the job wouldn't work out. I'd have to find some other work, but I had a place at school and a place to live. I left Parsons that day feeling better about my future than I had all summer.

I went home, packed my bags, and drove back to Parsons. That year I repeated classes from Metro JC and pulled in a 3.3 GPA, which was enough to allow me to transfer the next year to Pittsburg State, a four-year public college about 35 miles from Parsons.

My first year at Pitt State went reasonably well. My academic record remained mired in mediocrity, but at least I was passing. And at the same time I was having a lot of fun. My second semester I joined the Phi Sigma Epsilon fraternity, where I made a lot of good friends.

It was then that my college days were interrupted. It was 1967, and the Vietnam War was escalating. When I came home for the summer, my brother-in-law warned me that I had better do something militarily or I'd get drafted. That I did not want, so I went to the closest Army recruiting station and found that they had a classification for a lab technician. I signed up for a six-year commitment that included four years of reserve duty, and I went to basic training at Fort Polk in Louisiana. I also spent time at Brooke Army Hospital near San Antonio, Fitzsimons Army Hospital outside Denver, and finally at Fort Hood in central Texas.

The main job of my group was to draw blood, which earned us the moniker of "blood suckers." Most people had their blood drawn in the morning, so my afternoons were often used to help the pathologists with autopsies, which got me thinking I might actually be able to swing medical school like Mom had always dreamed. I rose to the level of staff sergeant during my time in the service, and after my active duty I returned to Pitt State and began pursuing a premed degree.

In retrospect, it was not the ideal major for someone who also wanted to party as much as I did.

I moved back into my old fraternity and began "mentoring" some new pledges. Eventually we were friends, helped along by the fact that they occasionally had access to my Mom's cooking. Any weekend I brought home friends, Mom would make the typical Jewish meal of brisket and chicken. There was enough food for 25 people, and when it was time to return to campus Mom would pack up the leftovers for us to take with us. My buddies, a lot of whom came to school from other parts of the country and weren't able to go home often, couldn't wait to get this food.

Though I may not have been the only Jewish kid on campus, I was certainly the only one in my fraternity. I wasn't going to temple at that time, but I did try to avoid pork and eat kosher and explain bits of my Jewish traditions, especially around special holidays. I never felt any animosity or discrimination from fellow students, friends, or girlfriends, and I was proud of my heritage.

At Pitt State there was a big event in the fall called Frontier Weekend, which was a Friday night hayride and Saturday night barn party south of the city. I needed a date. Steve Brace, one of my roommates and a pledge I had "mentored," suggested he fix me up on a blind date with a girl he'd met on campus — a pretty freshman cheerleader from Wichita named Paula Beebe. Their last names were close alphabetically, so they had sat close to each other in several classes and become friends. On the Wednesday night before the big event, we all decided to go to a show and get drinks afterward to give Paula and me a chance to get acquainted. I immediately liked her, but the feeling wasn't entirely mutual.

Although I was only a sophomore academically, I was three years older than she was, and after my tour in the service I thought had all the answers. The next day I heard from Steve that Paula liked me okay but thought I was a little cocky. Probably an understatement. Since she was already committed for the weekend, she would still go as my date, and I was determined to change her perception and make sure she had a good time. Between the hayride and the barn party we spent much of that weekend together, and, with a Herculean effort on my part to be my better self, she began to be able to see past my bravado.

We started dating in earnest and it didn't take long before I knew she was the one, so I worked hard to continue trying to impress her. I took a job at a men's store in town and traded out clothes for pay. After I left the service Dad had surprised me with a 1968 Pontiac GTO, and I kept it up beautifully. Along with my status as a premed major, I was looking good — on paper.

My grades continued to be average at best, however, and Mom had to finally accept the fact that I wasn't going to become a doctor. To her credit, she kept her disappointment to a minimum. As usual, Dad didn't really seem to care as much. At least he didn't talk about it with me. I had come to realize, though, that my parents supported me the best they knew how, each in their own unique way. My mom pushed me to pursue a goal beyond my reach but loved me just the same when I fell short of the mark. My dad watched from his vantage point on the sidelines, much as he had when I was a kid playing sports, quiet, but always dependably there.

Because of my time in the service and my earlier misadventures in junior college, I was nearly 25 when I graduated in 1971. True to my word with Dr. Keller, I had no plans for medical school. Honestly, I was just glad to be graduating. Though my relationship with Paula was still strong, I had little focus in any other aspect of my life.

I knew I owed a lot of people a great deal of gratitude for having made it this far. Even good old Dr. Keller had his share of putting me on a path toward a good (and nonmedical) future, though at 25 it was hard to see it. At the time I may have been at a loss to anticipate what was coming next, but, looking back, I can see I already had the tools I would need — a foundation of principles formed by the people and experiences that had already shaped me and shape me still.

Chapter 2
TURN ON YOUR IGNITION

Principle #2: Have a passion for
your profession and for life

*"The only way to do great work
is to love what you do."*

Steve Jobs

When I arrived home after college with (technically) a degree and no plan to speak of, I found my friends and family full of advice. Having enjoyed my time selling men's clothing in college, I had the general idea that I might be good at sales. So Dad suggested a route he was familiar with and, through his pharmacy connections, was able to get me a sales department interview at Marion Labs, the Kansas City pharmaceutical giant founded by Ewing Kauffman, the original owner of the Kansas City Royals. My buddy Larry Spitcaufsky suggested car sales, if only for the perk of having a car to drive. So, along with Marion Labs, I also applied to several local car dealerships. I had an interview or two that I thought went well, though the silence I received in return seemed to contradict that impression. I was beginning to get nervous.

Enter my Aunt Mary Greenstein. She'd never had children but took care of her nieces and nephews as if they were her own. She was a strong personality who always looked out for us, whether we asked for it or not. For 28 years she had worked as the office manager at the Shalom Geriatric Center, and through her job had made connections with a number of business leaders in the Kansas City area's Jewish community.

In 1971, one of her SGC residents was the mother of Leon Morse, co-owner of Clasen-Morse Chevrolet, which was among the dealerships I had applied to but had received no response. When Aunt Mary heard that I was trying to get in the car business, she got into Mr. Morse's ear and convinced him to give me a chance. Mr. Morse soon put me to work selling new cars.

I'll admit that, at the start, my heart wasn't really in it. Maybe I was still slightly mourning the loss of my future in medicine, maybe I wasn't as convinced as Larry was that this business was for me. Whatever the case, my results were adequate, but nothing special. In my restlessness, after only a few months at Clasen-Morse I had already made plans to try something else when I got a call from Frank Stinson.

Frank was the used car manager at Van Chevrolet, another established dealership across town. He had heard through a friend that I was planning on leaving Clasen-Morse and wanted to give me a chance at Van. He said that he saw potential in me and thought he could make something of it. Slightly inspired and a bit flattered, I decided to give car salesmanship another try with Frank's guidance.

Success was not immediate. In fact, the assistant manager at Van, a guy named Ron Huber, told me I might be better off going back to school and doing "the medical thing."

"You may not be cut out for the car business," he added.

His dig rankled. Whether it was his version of reverse psychology or just him being kind of a jerk, it was motivating. I had never wanted to prove someone wrong more.

Fortunately, I had a supporter in Frank, who liked me and took an interest in my work. Frank himself was an underdog success story. He had come to Kansas City from Arkansas with little to his name but had worked hard to achieve his position. He appreciated others around him who were willing to work hard, too.

Frank believed that I had the work ethic necessary for success in the car business and thought I could be a player, but something else needed to click. "You're a nice guy," he told me, "and you present yourself well. But you could be doing much better. I think you have what it takes to be good at this job, and if you're willing to work at it, I can show you how."

I assured him, with perhaps more certainty than I felt at that moment, that I did want to be a successful salesman and was ready to learn from him.

"The first thing you need," he said, "is to be more assertive with customers, more aggressive and outgoing on the sales floor, and more decisive. Act like you want to be there at least as much as your customers do."

Perhaps sensing my rising feeling of being in over my head, he gave me an encouraging smile. "Keep working and you'll make it happen."

Both Ron and Frank, each in their unique way, fired me up. Frank's advice had confirmed what I'd already suspected: I knew I needed to be more assertive, more persuasive — more passionate about what I was doing. So I made a decision to let go of other possibilities — doors that hadn't opened — and dedicate myself to this job.

About the same time, my relationship with Paula had reached a crossroads. She had been a year behind me in school but was approaching her own graduation in the spring of 1972. She had spent her senior year student teaching in her hometown of Wichita and coming up on weekends to stay with me and my parents in Kansas City.

One Saturday night we were sitting and talking in my car in my parents' driveway when Paula pointed out that she was about to graduate, which, of course, I knew. I could feel The Talk coming, but I had already thought about it and was ready. I knew — and had known for a long time — that I loved Paula and wanted to marry her. So, when she asked where we were going with our relationship, I asked her to give me another year to get established in my job.

Then there was a pause I couldn't account for. It had seemed like a reasonable thing to say, but something had clearly gone wrong.

She looked over at me and asked, "Is that the way you feel? Is that what you want to do?"

I knew I was on shaky ground but hadn't yet figured out why. "Yeah. Do you agree?"

She did not.

"If that's all you want, no. I'm out of here," she said. She opened the door and started walking to her car.

"Where are you going?"

"I'm going home. Obviously, this is not going to work."

Up until this point, whatever challenges I'd faced, I'd always felt like I could dance my way around most anything, figure out a way to finesse myself through any tough situation. That overconfident guy who had not particularly impressed Paula at our first meeting had been tempered but had never really gone away. And that guy was rather startled by this unexpected turn of events and was getting more worried by the moment.

In my sales training I had learned that in negotiations one tactic is to stay silent and let the other person do the talking. You make your statement or position known and then shut up, the idea being that the first person who talks is the one who gives in. But Paula had preempted my opportunity to shut up and this was far more important than negotiating a car sale. I loved this woman and did not want to watch her walk away from me and our relationship, A vision of my future without Paula flashed before me, and I knew I had to do or say something quickly. In my most persuasive voice I said, "Wait, wait. Maybe we ought to talk about this. What were *you* thinking about us?"

Paula has never been one to fly off the handle, and in her calm manner she responded (to my eternal relief), "I love you and I want to make a real future of this. But if you don't, that's your prerogative."

I realized then that the issue was, in her eyes, one of genuine commitment and passion. Soulless plans for jobs and wedding dates meant nothing without them, so I told her how I truly felt. Soon we started making wedding plans, and by August we were married.

• • • •

As I look back, that conversation with Paula in my parents' driveway in 1972 was my "Aha!" moment. What I'd begun to learn at the dealership had taken form and substance in my personal life as well. As I dedicated myself to this woman and to the profession I wanted to sustain us both, I realized I needed to have passion with a purpose and that need extended to all areas of life.

It's a principle I have continued to learn and have reinforced for me time and again over the years. Achieving my highest level of success required my highest level of commitment, and passion, in practical ways, often translates as devotion, time, and attention. This has applied to my occupation, certainly, but also to my daily life, my partner, my children, my family and friends, community work, even my own health and well-being.

This means that when I take on new activities or relationships, I do so with the intention of giving it my all. If I'm involved in an organization, I'm not going to do it simply to pad my résumé, it will be because I care about the cause. I'm going to give it my time, my full attention, and the best of my skill and effort. I'm going to be outspoken because my voice as an advocate matters. I may even ruffle feathers because I'm going to feel strongly about what I'm doing.

There is, of course, a difference between passionate outspokenness and being argumentative. We have all known people who were contentious seemingly for the sake of it and have felt the challenges of dealing with them. At the heart of any endeavor, however, must be a fundamental belief that there is something of value to accomplish and that it deserves to be done well. This is the difference between argument and advocate, between simply wanting to win or being right and making a difference in the world around you. It's the purpose that guides the passion and keeps it focused.

As a young, newly married car salesman, all of this changed how I looked at each customer. If the work was of value and every sale mattered, then so did every customer, every person that came into my sphere. So, while some of the other salespeople would prejudge customers as they came into the showroom, making little effort to wait on them if they looked unkempt or wore cheap clothing, I decided that every customer would get my complete attention and I waited on everyone I could.

This attention, born of passion for the task combined with my own parents' early teaching that all people were of value, showed the customers with whom I interacted that I respected them. In giving them my time, I showed that I respected theirs. In the end, a lot of those unkempt folks turned into buyers, and many became repeat customers.

Late one afternoon, not long after I'd decided to go all in with my effort at Van, a man walked onto the used car lot looking for a birthday present for his daughter. It was nearly closing time and not many salespeople were still around, but I had already made it my practice to stay as long as was needed to sell a potential customer a car, even if that meant I was the last person to leave for the day. I introduced myself and asked how I could help. We chatted about his daughter and what would suit her, his job, and the long hours he worked which had resulted in his late-in-the-day stop by the car lot. I made sure he knew that I was interested in him, not just a sale, and in making sure that he was satisfied with however our time ended, either with a car purchase or a decision to keep looking. As it turned out, we were quickly able to find something he liked and started the paperwork.

Sitting with him in the office, I noticed he wore a shirt that bore a logo for Kansas City Power & Light — the region's high-profile electric company. He gave me his business card, and I asked him what his job there was. When he told me he was the purchasing agent, which included the company's fleet of vehicles, I asked if I could take him to lunch and introduce him to our fleet manager who might be able to help him out the next time the company needed any new vehicles.

He was amenable to that, so later I asked my supervisor how I should proceed, ready to hand this potential fleet customer off to the proper department.

"Why don't you just handle it?" he asked. "Go out there and see what they're thinking and work on the deal yourself."

I agreed before he could change his mind and started thinking about what we had to offer KCP&L. I took him to lunch, discussed the deal, and we moved ahead in making Van Chevrolet the company's new fleet supplier. It wasn't a big commission for me (only about $50 per car), but it was a feather in my cap. I had shown the company that I could be assertive, that I cared about furthering the business and creating new customers, that I cared about my part of the whole.

Triumphs like these helped fuel my newfound passion. Yes, legwork and initiative were integral to such successes, and seeing that effort reap some dividends gave me confidence, but it all stemmed from that foundational devotion to give my full effort to the endeavor. I had found something I truly enjoyed, and I was steadily improving. I knew I had plenty more to learn, but I was beginning to feel more confident that I could make it in the car business and be more than just average.

For a ready example I needed to look no farther than the dealership's owner, Cecil Van Tuyl. Cecil grew up a farm kid in La Cygne, Kansas, who, after a stint in the Navy near the end of WWII, moved to Kansas City for a welding job at the General Motors plant. After a few years on the assembly line, Cecil decided it would be better to sell cars than to build them. He started working on a used car lot, then worked for a Studebaker dealer, but he soon opened his own used car business. He steadily expanded it while at the same time buying last year's models that were still new off other dealers' lots and flipping them for profit. He had an appetite and a talent for selling, and before too long General Motors noticed all the hard work and natural sales ability of its old employee. GM put him up in his first dealership in Kansas City in 1955, and he named it Van Chevrolet. He later took over a struggling store in Quincy, Illinois, and about the same time bought a third dealership in Topeka, Kansas. In 1961, he moved the KC operation to Merriam, Kansas, near I-35, where I first met him.

Cecil had a work ethic that was second to none and he expected the same from his employees. Though his expectations were high, he treated us well. He liked to hire young people and develop their skills, to put them in management positions to see if they had the talent and, more importantly, the passion, to be successful. If he liked what he saw and those individuals could prove themselves, he would give them ownership opportunities in his dealerships as he continued to expand across the country. When the family sold a controlling stake in the company to Berkshire Hathaway for $4.1 billion in 2015, it was among the top five largest dealership networks in the country (and the largest that was privately owned), with 78 stores and nearly $8 billion in annual revenue. His formula obviously worked. In time, I would be one of those who would benefit from this business model.

Just as Paula, Frank, Cecil, and others helped me learn the value — the necessity — of choosing my own path with passion, be it personal or professional, from Cecil I also learned the skill and importance of leading by example and helping others learn to create and pursue their passion. This capacity to identify and develop passion in others was one of the greatest skills Cecil taught me, and it took me years to come close to being as good at it as he was. In most fields, managers are trained for the technical aspects of their jobs. In a car dealership this means scheduling, budgeting, closing deals, working the desk, marketing, advertising, dealer trading, and other related skills.

What is most challenging, however, is training someone in the intangibles — how to motivate, how to set expectations, how to identify talent and draw it out, how to communicate a vision. But these are the elements that make managers able to lead their teams into becoming a passionate workforce.

While one fully committed person can be powerful, an organization's real strength is seen when that commitment is shared by a team or even a whole workforce. Cecil had figured out how to do that, and he led by example. As a result, he made a lot of people successful. At the core of it were two basic tenets: treat people right and show them that you care. Do these two things and your own passion will begin to take root in those over whom you have influence.

I have seen passion become a driver of ambition and provide inspiration for higher accomplishment, and I have seen the lack of passion leach the joy out of work that could have become purposeful. When hiring and promoting I try to identify passion, but it is not an easy task. You make a choice and hope it's the right one. If not, it doesn't take long to determine when a person doesn't possess that trait and has no desire to acquire it. I once hired a service manager who was recommended from another organization to run my body shop. I asked him what he knew about body shops, and he convinced me that his management experience and skills were enough to be transferable to a new department.

Ninety days into the job, however, I could see the passion wasn't there, and I hadn't been able to draw it out of him. In the end I decided to replace him with an assistant who had already been in that department for several years and cared for the people and the processes we had in place — in other words, someone who I knew already had passion for the work. It was the right choice. Hiring somebody with experienced indifference wasn't as good as the assistant with green willingness. The managerial skills he learned as he needed to, his learning curve leveled out a bit by his desire to do well, and he did the job successfully and effectively for years.

Ultimately, passion does not — cannot — ensure material success, though it can sometimes open doors to that sort of opportunity. And the lack of passion doesn't automatically prevent a person from being productive, though it can make it more of a struggle to be so. As this idea of passion was for me, a slightly adrift new college graduate who needed direction and purpose, so it is for all of us — a decision. Will we choose what to follow, will we choose what drives us, or will we be pushed by circumstances that aim to keep us adrift?

The real benefit of living a passion-filled life and encouraging those around us to do the same is seen best in our wake. What do we leave behind us as we go? The answer to this question should motivate us to improve our own little corners of the world and to leave something of value behind when our time is finished. For my part, I hope I leave behind people who knew they mattered to me and were themselves encouraged to move forward in their own lives with purpose and passion.

Chapter 3
DRIVING FOR THE LONG HAUL

Principle #3: Make it more than a job; make it a lifetime

"Whatever you are, be a good one."
William Makepeace Thackeray

When Frank Stinson from Van Chevrolet called me in 1972 to discuss employment opportunities, he asked why I was leaving Clasen-Morse.

"I need to get myself a career," I said. "This is just a job."

"I think I can give you a career," he told me.

Frank saw me as the right kind of person for the industry, and he gave me a chance to stay in the game even when I was struggling. At Van, I became a pretty good salesman, moving about 15 or so cars a month. Though my numbers were decent, however, they were nowhere near our top producers who were closing about 40 sales a month. Those guys were laser-focused on just moving cars, and that's all they ever wanted to do. I, on the other hand, had decided to set my sights on management.

Though I was still figuring out just what differentiated a job from a career, I knew I wanted to try roles in the dealership other than that of a salesperson.

After some of my early successes I was given more responsibility, and my efforts were being noticed by supervisors throughout the organization, including Cecil Van Tuyl. In June 1974, I moved into my first management position in the finance division, and over the next four years I became a manager in both the new and used car departments.

The personal financial rewards were starting to come as well, and that coincided with the growth of our family. Paula and I had settled in the Kansas City area, and she taught school for a few years before our daughters were born — Mandi in 1976 and Allison in 1978. The same year Ali was born, I was also named the general manager of the dealership. I was promoted at a time of some disarray for that particular store, so I immediately faced challenges requiring a great deal of time and attention.

I also began learning a few new things about Cecil's management style as our professional relationship changed. We would open the doors to the showroom at 8:00 a.m., but the service department opened at 6:30 so customers could drop off their cars. Cecil's offices were nearby, and he would often stop by the dealership on his way in to check things out. One morning early on I got there about 7:30, and Cecil was waiting on the service drive. The next morning, I decided to get there at 7:15 and be ahead of him, but there he was, already waiting on the service drive. The following day I went in at 7:00 and there he sat. I began to wonder when or if Cecil ever slept, and I toyed with the idea that he was simply camping on the service drive.

In any case, this seemed to be a contest I was losing, and I determined that I would now start arriving at 6:30, but for the next several days Cecil wasn't there when I drove in. In fact, he didn't show up at all. It turned out he'd gone to Phoenix with his wife and conveniently forgotten to mention it. After a couple weeks of the non-Cecil routine, I'd settled into an arrival time around 7:00 or 7:15 — only to unexpectedly find him waiting for me again one morning on the service drive. Determined not to be outdone this time, I immediately pushed my arrival time back to 6:30, only to discover that he had left town again.

Over time, I came to understand that Cecil's early morning appearances weren't due to his lack of trust about my ability to do the job or a propensity toward being manipulative. He just wanted to see that I was being conscientious and consistent, and I soon made the determination that I would get there each morning at 7:00, whether or not anyone was there to check up on me. In his own style, Cecil was trying to teach me that to be focused on a career it was imperative to understand the workday didn't just begin when the doors opened to the public. Preparation and dedication to the task at hand were essential. The minutes were never the point, but the attitude was, and arriving early was one practical way to show an attitude that was invested in the business and in the work.

Conversely, those who come to work right before their scheduled start time may be doing their job, but they're likely just doing the minimum. They're probably not doing their most productive work, nor are they interested in enhancing their opportunities for advancement. I always tell my people, "Don't just show up." And it's still attitude and preparedness that serve as the foundation of that idea. People who are trying to excel and establish themselves are ready for each day, each shift. Even something as simple as arriving to work early to log on to their computers and be ready at the appointed hour can make a difference. In truth, a person could arrive early every day and still waste the time. Instead, those looking for something greater will use whatever time is available to cultivate an awareness of what's going on and be focused and ready to meet whatever is coming next. This mindset begins to differentiate between those who come to work to do a job and those who come looking for a career.

Likewise, as a business owner it is inherent that I treat my people right and help provide motivation. Common sense dictates that when people are treated well — employees as well as customers — and business is done ethically, it's much easier for employees and customers alike to respect the business and feel good about putting their own valuable resources into it. Without that foundational respect, there is little chance of success of virtually any kind.

The difference between a job and a career, in the end, comes down to the difference in pursuing short-term goals versus long-term goals. In a job, people work in the short-term for a paycheck to make enough money to support their needs, and they are compensated in exchange for performing a specified set of duties and completing them on schedule. They may be hourly or on salary, have a required set of hours or a flexible schedule. They can work in large companies, small businesses, or even be self-employed.

A career, on the other hand, results from a long-term outlook fueled by passion, which is the integral component of achievement. A career is a journey steered by goals and ambitions, and when successful will hopefully bring not only monetary rewards, but also the often longer-lasting and more formative benefits of pride, satisfaction, and a sense of self-worth. A career spans a lifetime, and can be with the same organization or many, in one field or across industries.

As ever, it's an individual's outlook that makes the real difference — an outlook based on the aspiration to make their job a career or find a new job that can become one. They need to identify their passion (there's that word again) and pursue it. But often that entails taking some risk, and that can be a difficult decision when faced with the possibility of forgoing a paycheck indefinitely in order to pursue a new path. These fears are real and practical and are at the heart of why many people are unwilling or unable to get out of their ruts and not push the boundaries of their potential.

Transforming a job into a career involves a choice. My parents and mentors taught me that God gave us the ability to think, to love, to create, to plan, and to imagine, but the greatest gift He gave us was the power to choose. We can choose what attitude we want, and we can succeed if we have the heart and soul to care and are supported by people who also care. A successful career results from a combination of attitude, care, hard work, and planning, then keeping on track with that plan and changing it with the times as needed.

Pursuing a career — the keeping on track part — also requires discipline. It's easy to desire a career and state a bunch of goals, and many can figure out how to stick with a goal for a little while, but it's discipline that makes long-term goals genuinely achievable. It's what keeps us productive. It mandates scheduling, prioritizing, and avoiding distractions. Yes, it's important to earn that paycheck so that we can live from day-to-day. But it's also crucial for the achiever to chart a path for where he or she intends to go.

I was fortunate in that I always had a support system around me as I was making these decisions, particularly the ones early in my career. I had family and friends who knew me well giving me good advice and helping me find jobs. I had Paula, from the very beginning, as a partner in the choices I made. She and the girls gave me daily motivation and drive. Without that support, I don't know what my path would have looked like, but it would have been quite different. Even later on, people like Cecil, who had only known me in business, would become part of my support system, helping me find my way through difficult times.

The importance of such support cannot be overstated. It's true that there are people who somehow manage to fight through adversity and challenges seemingly on their own, but they are the remarkable exceptions that prove the rule. The vast majority of us need other people in our corner, if only to know that we have something to fight for. We do them and ourselves a disservice when we fail to acknowledge that or when we take them for granted. I'm also fortunate that when I was sometimes guilty of taking my support system for granted, they loved and cared for me anyway.

Whatever the support system you're able to gather around you, creating a career is not a quick process. Managing a job versus a career can be compared to short-term versus long-term life strategies. Working for your regular wage is really a reflection of a short-term plan. That steady paycheck can actually demotivate an individual from focusing on career goals. It's true that life barrels forward, and obligations and responsibilities need to be met. That is simply reality. But at the same time, the career-oriented individual puts their own long-term plan in place. Practical individuals will keep this plan flexible, knowing that the future is abundant with changes, and adaptation will be necessary as they go.

I was fortunate early on that the Van Tuyl organization was structured in a way to encourage associates to develop careers.

Many of the people hired by Cecil stayed with the company for decades — some as many as 40 years. The business model incentivized, rewarded, and motivated. When Cecil opened one of his early dealerships in the 1960s, he began to cut people in on ownership. His strategy of developing talent and then making them partners and part-owners was based on the idea that they would do a better job of looking after and growing a business they had a stake in. He would even loan them the money to buy into the dealership. He would start them at a 25 percent ownership interest, and, if they were successful, that number would increase over time to the point that eventually they could buy Cecil out of his share. It was a highly motivating business model.

My opportunity to take part in it came along in 1979. I had done well in my first general manager position and had improved the performance of that Kansas City dealership. Cecil had dealerships all around the Kansas City area and in Illinois, and eventually we decided a store in Decatur, Illinois, made the most sense for my next opportunity. Decatur is a small city of about 70,000 people, 40 miles east of Springfield and 40 miles southwest of Champaign, which is the home of the University of Illinois. Paula was willing to go as well, so I jumped in. I needed $250,000 to buy in for 25 percent, of which I had $30,000. Cecil loaned me the rest. Our girls were six months and two years old when we packed up and moved five hours away. We were sorry to lengthen the distance from our families, but we realized this was a special opportunity.

Even at this stage of my career, after I had proven myself to the point that he made me a partner in one of his business ventures, Cecil maintained a watchful eye on my methods and career progress. He would only come to visit in person about every six months, but he had his ways to keep tabs on me from almost 400 miles away. He did still own 75 percent of the dealership after all.

Our Saturday closing time in Decatur was at 6:00 p.m. On one Saturday afternoon, I left the dealership at 4:30 to get ready for a party Paula and I were attending that night. When I came in on Monday, there was a message from Cecil for me at the switchboard, left at 5:55 p.m. on Saturday. He said he was calling to say hi, which was certainly true, but I knew Cecil well enough by then to know his various ulterior motives. He was calling to see if I was still at the office. I knew he would likely never say anything about it — he'd just put it in his memory bank and bring it back to mind should he ever have cause to assess my methods or motivation. I put it in my memory bank as well, and I thought twice before leaving early again.

This worked to continue to motivate me on my career path, though I still had a lot to learn about balancing a family and a profession in those days, and my successes often came on the backs of sacrifices made by my family. But I was still a young man with a lot of years for growth ahead of me, and I knew if I embraced this opportunity in this company there would be significant rewards. And there were. In Decatur I was hitting targets and earning bonuses. I was now part of Cecil's inner sanctum.

Reflecting on those early days with the Van Tuyl organization, I realize how professionally lucky I was that Cecil and his lieutenants had laid the foundation for me to have a satisfying and prosperous career. I see so many people who, for whatever reason, have only had jobs, and never a career. They feel underutilized, or they don't feel they can pursue their dreams and goals out of obligation or fear of losing a paycheck. Their hearts and their minds are elsewhere.

Smart managers also must understand that they need to do more than simply pay people in order for them to succeed and be inspired to pursue a career, and that employee successes translate into success for the entire business. Bonuses tied to achieving set goals can provide motivation, but a basic salary or hourly wage alone does not often provide much incentive beyond the minimum effort. A company can pay people to come to work to sit in a chair and input information into a computer, to answer phones, to fix engines, or do any other task, but unless they are given the motivation and tools to seek a career, the organization may be settling for corporate mediocrity as well as employee indifference.

Personally, once I have identified a talented individual, one whose attitude meshes well with mine and the rest of the team's, I want to give them every incentive to develop their job into a career, and then influence them to pursue that career within my organization. I try to develop them and keep them focused on long-term goals even when they may be bogged down by their daily routine. In my management style, the critical component for inspiration and motivation is to show people that I care. This means developing effective relationships with my staff members, so that I understand their individuality and what type of feedback and rewards give them the most encouragement. Each person on my staff has different needs, and thus it is not effective for a manager to use the same approach across the board to discipline or to show appreciation. By making the effort to spend quality time with staff, I can come to understand what makes each one of them unique and how best to motivate them.

No matter the method of incentivizing, it is incumbent on me as an effective manager to take the time to show gratitude to my staff members for their contributions to the organization as often as possible. In conjunction with that, I want to encourage continuous learning and career development among my associates. More than just being a manager, I must also be a mentor. This keeps the group engaged and develops a team mentality.

While my primary method of improving performance is with positive reinforcement, I have more subtle ways to make sure employees and managers stay focused and are productive — much in the manner of my mentor, Cecil Van Tuyl, though hopefully a little less passive-aggressive. As an owner and manager, it is necessary that I not be confined to my office. I spend a good deal of my day walking around the dealership talking to staff, making sure everything is in good order, and addressing any needs or concerns they might have. It sends a message to my crew that I care about them, but it also affords me some chances to set a good example for how business should be done. This kind of positive attitude and determination to do my best work can invigorate a business and help bring success.

So, if I'm walking through the showroom and I see a customer who hasn't been helped, I'll walk up to them, introduce myself as the owner, and ask them what I can do for them. If my salespeople see me waiting on a customer, the guilt at missing someone quickly begins to set in. They may come up and see if they can help, but I'll tell them, "I've got this one," and I'll see the customer through the entire process. A sale has been made and the customer leaves satisfied, and my employees see that not even the boss is above that basic, foundational principle of caring for customers moment by moment. They see in concrete terms the values I espouse and the energy I want to see from everyone there. The fact that no salesperson has earned a commission on that sale also makes an impression.

The message gets through. A friend who occasionally stops by the dealership once told me that every time he comes in the door there is somebody there to open it for him, greet him, and see what they might do to assist. Even when he's just stopping by for a social visit, it leaves him with a positive impression of our operation.

Managers may assume that all candidates have the same motivation and desire for a career, but realistically, it is only a minority who do. If a manager can detect in the hiring process that the person is just looking for a job and not a career, he or she probably won't hire them. And of those who are hired in our business, only one or two of every 10 will stick. This is particularly true on the sales side.

I can usually tell in a week or two whether a new hire is going to make it. The other managers and I must do our part to make sure each new person is supported and has proper training, but beyond that it's up to the individual to begin to develop a positive attitude and work steadily toward achieving their quotas and goals. A manager also must take care that everyone on the team has the same drive to reach the group's collective goals. A collection of individuals working hard may be able to accomplish a great deal, but eventually personal goals and motivations will come into conflict with those of other individuals and the larger organization, and someone who puts their own goals above those of the group has the ability to bring everyone down.

Though to an individual it can seem counterintuitive to place the success of the group above their own goals, it's really just another form of short-term versus long-term thinking, but on a larger scale. That's why a key component of a career focus is the desire to improve the whole organization and make it profitable in its entirety. For a business to be sustainable, certainly the bottom line must be positive, but the more profitable the company is the more rewards there are to share with the employees. This long-term focus benefits the group, and a byproduct of that collective success is even more individual achievement.

In the end, anything to which you have made a commitment can be a career. When I was first starting out, I made a commitment to sell cars, and many years later as the owner of a dealership, I'm still doing it. While I have had my own dealerships for many years now, they have all been offshoots of my original partnership with Van Tuyl, and it feels like I have been with the same group since that day that Frank Stinson first called. It didn't take me long, even when I was young and still a bit naïve, to see that it was an organization worth committing to and, as I was committed to them, I was fortunate that they remained committed to me. Their support and my family's support helped turn a job I took while waiting to figure out the rest of my life into a career that has shaped my life.

DALE BACKS AND THE BENCH

When **I** went to Decatur in 1979, the parts manager at the dealership I took over was a young man named Dale Backs. Dale was in his late 20s, and he was a hard-working farm boy from Shelbyville, Illinois. His father, Harry, went by his middle name Dale, so our Dale was called Sonny.

It was apparent to me soon after I arrived that this was a special guy. I promoted him up the ranks to used car manager, and later I made him the general manager of the Crown Oldsmobile-Toyota organization. Dale wanted to be in the front end of the business and eventually own his own dealership, and I wanted to help him achieve that goal.

Dale became a good friend, though he was kind of a quiet, introverted man who liked to keep his personal life to himself. One time when I tried to provide some counsel to him on a private matter, he quietly and firmly let me know that it was not my business. But he worked extremely hard, and people liked and respected him.

When I headed back to Kansas City as a partner in the Auto Plaza, I told him at some point I would bring him along to Kansas City, and we'd look for a store for him. But when we sold that dealership the next year, I told Dale to stay in Decatur a while longer, as I had nothing to offer him at the time. Then I bought the dealerships in Lawrence, and in October 1994 he moved to Kansas to become my general manager.

While he was known as Sonny in Decatur, we began calling him by his given name of Dale when he came to Lawrence. Before we purchased it, the dealership was known as Sonny Hill Motors, and we wanted no confusion with that name since "Sonny Hill" had been a pseudonym for the previous owner who'd had a less than stellar reputation. But Dale settled in easily and quickly became involved in the Lawrence community, serving as a trustee for his church among other activities.

I put Dale in charge of the day-to-day management of the dealerships. I would hold department meetings on a regular basis, but he was the guy who did most of the hiring and firing, and he would do his best to handle the irate customers himself instead of pulling me into it. He was a master at appeasing people who were upset and pleasing them before they got that way. He was a big reason we were winners of multiple Toyota President's Awards.

I sold him 10 percent of the stock in Crown Automotive to make him my partner, and we worked on a succession plan, so if all went well I'd sell him the remaining stock in the Lawrence stores when I was ready to retire. If something opened up beforehand within the region, though, he knew I'd also help him take advantage of that opportunity.

But in November 2010, Dale's wife, who was a nurse practitioner, called to tell me that he had some sort of cold or a virus, which they thought was causing a lower intestinal issue. It turned out to be something much worse — he had pancreatic cancer. He went to M.D. Anderson in Houston for treatments, and when he was back in town he would try to come to work.

But it was obvious he was in great discomfort, and I would send him home.

By April of the following year, Dale was gone. His wife called me the day he died, and I went over to their house right away. He had already passed, but I leaned over and kissed him goodbye as my way of bringing closure to a relationship that had lasted 32 years. He was only 60. I was grief-stricken.

I wanted to do something to honor Dale, who had done so much to help me grow my business and who was so admired by everyone at our dealerships and in the community. There's a not-for-profit organization in Lawrence called Van Go, Inc., which serves at-risk teenagers through the creation of public art projects and job training. Among their initiatives is a program called Benchmark, in which an aspiring artist works with a local business to design and create a custom bench.

The Crown dealerships have been a supporter of Van Go for several years, and we help them out by having our body shop annually apply Klear Kote finishes to preserve the benches. In honor of Dale's legacy, I decided to commission them to do a bench, which was designed and painted by a young woman named Mya Frazier and is on prominent display in our lobby. I plan to build a memorial garden outside of our dealership and put the bench there for the public to see. It could never be enough, but it's a comfort to be able to share this small piece of my friend with the world.

Chapter 4
THERE ARE NO SHORTCUTS

Principle #4: Don't cut corners

"If you do the work, you get rewarded.
There are no shortcuts in life."
Michael Jordan

It's long gone now, but when I was in high school my friends and I liked to frequent the popular Leawood Drive-In in south Kansas City. One night, Larry and I along with a few others decided to take his Nash Metropolitan convertible, a very subcompact car, and head to the drive-in. There were four or five of us wanting to go in this tiny car, a tight squeeze in the best of circumstances, but I also decided to be very clever and crawled in the trunk to save on the admission fee. We went through the entrance and started hitting a bunch of bumps, with me stuffed in the trunk like a clown in a circus car. In retrospect, I wonder if that wasn't where the roots of my claustrophobia began to take hold. In any case, I yelled at Larry to stop and park so I could get out, and I hit the latch to open the trunk. I had nearly finished unfolding myself when I looked up to see a security guard smiling down at me.

"Boys, welcome to the drive-in," he said. "We're glad you came to see the show, but I'm afraid it's time to head on out. Can I show you to the exit?"

Thus ended our night at the drive-in. It was a common enough dodge, a shortcut around the system, one that seldom worked, to be honest, but one that rarely had any lasting consequences in trying to cut that corner.

By 1974, I like to think that I had matured a bit, and I was trying to get ahead in the auto business as a young salesman, when I began to learn that lesson anew. I had plenty of chances to observe peers who were inclined to do their jobs the easy way, to cut a corner here or there, salespeople who embraced shortcuts, and I didn't want to follow in that path.

It happened that in those days my commute took me through a construction site where U.S. Route 69 was being expanded in the Kansas suburbs southwest of Kansas City. It was a long-term project, and over time I noticed a lot of old cars and pickup trucks parked onsite. These belonged to the workers, who I figured were probably making some pretty good money on a job this big and this lengthy. I suspected there was the potential for multiple car sales here, and I was determined to introduce myself.

Now, I have always prided myself in my appearance, but I knew that showing up on the site in a suit and tie was unlikely to help me connect to anyone there. It could even backfire completely and make it seem like I was trying to look like I considered myself above them. It's important to know your audience and make them feel comfortable, so one morning I put on a t-shirt and jeans, stopped at the construction trailer, and struck up a conversation with the foreman, a guy named Jimmy McKinney. We hit it off immediately.

A few days later I made arrangements with Jimmy to bring lunch to the crew. I went to McDonald's and bought bags of hamburgers and fries along with some sodas, and I took lunch to the site for all the workers and handed out my business cards while I was there, and we sat around and talked about cars over burgers and fries. On a couple of other occasions, I brought some cases of beer over at quitting time, which gave us even more of an opportunity to visit. I didn't know if they really had extra spending money or not or if anyone was even in the market for a car — I was just trying to develop relationships. I certainly hoped they'd stop by the showroom, but the truth was I was enjoying getting to know them.

As it turned out, over the course of the next few weeks, my efforts resulted in the sale of 25 cars, including a new Corvette for Jimmy McKinney.

These sales came about because I did my homework, and I made myself accessible. I made an extra, genuine effort to connect with the workers in a place and in a way in which they felt comfortable, and I considered how I could develop a rapport with them. This was obviously long before we had access to the abundance of information on the internet, so I had to use my own observations and intuition that these workers could be prospects in the first place. I even made a couple of calls to learn more about the project — how big it was and when it was expected to be completed. Free food always enticing, and bringing them a meal gave me a chance to visit while we ate. People learn a lot about each other over the breaking of bread — or of French fries, or while sharing a cold beer. They came to trust me and to know I would be fair in selling them a car.

Unlike my Leawood drive-in experience, I didn't take any shortcuts. My approach to this opportunity required a comprehensive process and a plan.

The other young sales guys who did try to do it the easy way seldom lasted long, and it was no surprise they didn't make it. It was easy to sit in the dealership and wait for someone to come in the door, and on a busy Saturday even a mediocre salesperson might sell four or five cars. But there were plenty of slow days, especially during those times in the 1970s when the economy was stagnant and interest rates were high, and a busy weekend here and there wouldn't be enough to keep anyone going for long.

We learned early on you need to talk to 10 to 20 people to generate five legitimate prospects, and of that five, four would probably walk away. That's a lot of folks to encounter to sell one car, and that's when I understood I'd have to work hard at this. It would take an organized, consistent prospecting plan to distinguish myself. Instead of sitting and waiting for business to come in the door, I began calling everyone I could and going door-to-door at local businesses to hand out my business cards. It was exhausting and it was challenging, but it was what I had to do.

I also made it a point to wait on every customer I could, regardless of whether or not they immediately seemed like likely buyers. Sometimes this effort paid off and sometimes not, but it was an important habit to develop. I didn't want to use stereotypes to take shortcuts in how I judged people who walked into the dealership. My determination to avoid this propensity actually led to my first sale with Van Chevrolet.

It was 1971 and I was still very green, when a young guy saw a souped up, high-performance Camaro sitting in our lot and walked in the dealership. The older guys didn't like to wait on the younger folks because they assumed they weren't serious buyers. When I asked if I could help him, he said, "I want that car." He didn't want to test drive it. He didn't want to look under the hood. He didn't even want to kick the tires. He was single-minded about that Camaro and gave me a check for $1,000 as a deposit. My heart started fluttering — could this be the first real transaction I completed for my new employer? I got him approved for a loan for the balance, and when he came back to pick up the car, I was still a little worried he would change his mind. He hadn't even started the engine yet!

When he did, though, everyone on the lot knew it. The engine in that Camaro was nearly drag racer-ready, and when he turned the key in the ignition the noise rattled the windows.

He smiled. "Thanks. This is exactly what I want."

He happily drove off the lot, and I was hardly less happy as I watched (and listened) to him go, more pleased with every passing minute that I hadn't taken the shortcut of believing in stereotypes.

• • • •

Success in the long-term is like training for a marathon, and there are no shortcuts. Preparing for a marathon requires work on an almost daily basis, the perseverance to fight through setbacks from inevitable injuries and pain, and the patience to deal with outside factors like weather that are beyond the runner's control. And each day of training has its own goal and plan, and all those smaller goals serve the larger aim of a race well-run.

So it is in business. It is essential to practice and improve skills regularly, to overcome the inevitable days of failure, and to deal with the effects of uncontrollable factors such as a fluctuating economy or government regulations. And patience is a mandatory trait. No one wakes up one morning and finds that overnight they have magically become triumphant. Form a plan, avoid the tempting shortcuts, and take it one step at a time. Each step, each shorter-term daily plan, brings you that much closer to your long-term goals.

Fortunately for my own career development, I was able to study and acquire necessary skills for my progress on the job. The sales team at Van Chevrolet was regularly sent to seminars and training classes, but the best learning experiences I had come from being around some pretty good salespeople day after day. I made it a point to observe the veteran salespeople in action, ask them questions, and in any way possible learn whatever I could from them. We had an open floor plan, with partitions separating our work areas, so I was also able to eavesdrop on the other salespeople during their conversations with customers and prospects — both in person and on the phone.

There were two veteran salesmen I watched particularly closely. Both regularly sold 40 cars per month, which was a spectacular total. One was a bulldog who wouldn't take no for an answer from a prospective buyer. He would press and press, sometimes intimidating the purchaser in the process, until he had made a sale. Then he would turn that buyer over to the finance department to complete the paperwork, and from that moment on he was completely done with the transaction. He was so ready to move on to the next sale that when people would return to pick up their vehicles, he often wouldn't even remember their names.

The second salesman had a completely different style. He was a dapper guy who always wore a hat and tie — very nattily dressed. He would greet customers warmly, make them feel comfortable, and keep their names on file so he could follow up. He saw the sales process through from start to finish and garnered a lot of repeat business.

Two different sales methods from two very different people, but both were productive in their own unique ways. I determined that I could learn from both and become a sort of hybrid between these two veterans. Like the bulldog, I could be more aggressive in meeting and greeting potential buyers as they entered the showroom floor, but I could also follow up and earn their respect so that they would be repeat customers. I wanted to be the complete package.

Through observation and osmosis, I was able to carve out my own style, and I like to think that because of my brief flirtation with a medical career I had a good bedside manner that translated well into sales. That helped me in the business, because many customers walking through the door thought all salespeople just wanted to get in their pocket and nothing more. I developed the skill of generating a rapport and putting them at ease.

Though I never reached an average of 40 cars a month, I became a consistent performer, and I did well enough to impress the supervisors, including Cecil Van Tuyl. They thought I could be successful in a management position in time, and they began helping me gain the skills and experience that would make that possible.

Cecil himself was the perfect exemplar of someone who had not taken shortcuts. His story was compelling, and it was filled with bumps in the road, especially in the early days of his career. But he had a vision, a determination to see it through, and a plan to make it happen. And his success wasn't limited to his automotive dealerships. He flourished in real estate investment and development and also had an interest in marinas. When someone once told him he had the Midas touch, he responded, "Midas touch? Hell, behind that desk, working day and night, that's how I earned what I have."

Even with such a strong example to learn from, it was easy to slip into corner-cutting bad habits. When I was just starting out in sales, I too had fallen into the practice of waiting for customers to walk in the door. That obviously wasn't going to work to maintain a steady income during slow times, or, more importantly, fulfill my commitment to a long-term career. It was a habit I had to break. I learned that you had to have a plan for each transaction and each day that would help push you toward long-term goals.

Some of the other young salespeople, tasked with looking for new prospects, would pick a name and a number, sometimes at random, just to be able to say they'd called someone. It was technically true, but they were basically throwing darts at a board and hoping they might connect sometime. There was no strategy or design in their efforts.

When I felt I had a serious prospect I had a plan to help move them toward a decision. I tried to get a feel for their needs and where they were in the sales process. If they showed reluctance or discomfort in negotiating, I did my best to make them comfortable and not let myself fall back into any stereotypical car sales tactics. Other folks just walked in the showroom and wanted the best bottom-line price we could offer. With so many dealerships in the Kansas City area they might make their decision on a $25 or $50 difference in price, so I'd try to slow them down and see how I could differentiate our dealership from the competition. While every prospective customer was a little different, as I learned more and planned more, I became better equipped to address each unique situation.

These short-term strategies for making contacts and caring for customers augmented my larger plan for success — one that I hoped would help achieve lifetime goals. Without those long-term goals it would have been easy for my career and life to become one of confusion and distraction. Such goals and planning need to strike a proper balance between personal and professional needs and must include input from family members who are directly impacted by your choices.

Once those goals are set, the plan can be fine-tuned. It's a good idea to commit the plan to writing — make it concrete and real — and revisit it periodically to make changes. Times change, and there are bound to be unanticipated roadblocks and obstacles. There will be family issues, which should always take top priority, and unforeseen events in the outside world that can dramatically affect your business. These will require modification and maybe even a complete change in the end goals — some may no longer be attainable while others may mandate a deferred timeline. The key is to understand there will be problems and challenges along the way. Trying to shortcut around them or ignore their effects will often result in failure.

I faced the need to reassess and make goal changes from the very beginning of my career. During 1973 and '74, after I had only been in the business a couple of years, the Organization of Petroleum Exporting Companies (better known as OPEC) imposed an oil embargo against the United States and other countries in retaliation for their support of Israel during the Arab-Israeli Yom Kippur War. This caused an upward spiral in oil prices, a gas shortage, and long lines at the pumps. Auto sales were obviously negatively affected, so I quickly had to shift my focus to making significantly more contacts to reach my sales goals, and also shift sales toward economy cars, since there was suddenly a limited appetite for gas guzzlers.

A few years later, I had reached the level of new car manager and thought I was in line to become the general manager of Van Chevrolet. Cecil didn't think I was ready, and, although he was probably right, it still irritated me. In retrospect I think he was testing me. Either way, the goal I was reaching for had been deferred by the decisions of others and I had to adjust. In the end, Cecil hired an outsider from Wichita, and the guy was basically a hatchet man. He managed through fear, firing a significant number of people in management and sales and ordering me to get 25 new salespeople on staff or I would be "going away." I could have quit, found a job at another dealership, or done my regular level of work and let the chips fall where they may, but I knew, even in my irritation, that the best path forward was still with the Van Tuyl organization, so I worked round the clock and managed to meet those high expectations. I even won over that general manager as well. Soon after, he told me that he wanted out of our company, and he could help make sure I'd be in line for his job when he left. Eventually, he departed for another dealership, and in February 1978 I was finally promoted to the general manager's position.

I knew I was in the right place at the right time and felt confident in how I was performing, but there were more obstacles to traverse, more shifts in the long-term goals that would require planning and no shortcuts. Our previous boss had left me an organization with low morale and an underperforming staff, and I spent my initial days in the new position settling everyone down.

About six months into the job Cecil came to me and said, "Good work. Now how about making some money?" The message was clear — the morale goal had been achieved and it was time to refocus — so I set out to hire the best people I could find, and we soon began to turn a profit again.

By the next year I had just taken over the Decatur store, in which I had an ownership interest, and was again tasked with turning around an operation. To complicate matters, the U.S. economy was in a period of "stagflation," characterized by high interest rates and unemployment. If I continued doing business the way the previous manager had in Decatur we'd lose money, because once again demand for new cars was soft. I had to modify the compensation plan of the sales staff so they would be incentivized to do a better job — a higher risk, higher reward type of structure. If they did more business the dealership and the individual salesperson would make more money. I lost some people, but the dealership succeeded and those who stayed were rewarded.

The bottom line was that I had to change with the times and those changes required setting goals and an adherence to a plan for meeting those goals that wasn't looking for only the quickest or easiest solutions. Instead, even when easier or quicker methods were available, I had to be willing to choose the harder work, the measure of sacrifice, the long view that would help create firm foundations for future success, for myself certainly, but also for those who depended upon me and the organization that we all relied upon.

Things shifted again when Cecil gave me the opportunity to move back to Kansas City in 1991. I had been in Decatur for 12 years and thought I would never return because of the competitive nature of the Kansas City auto market. My girls were now 14 and 12 and remembered nothing but Decatur. We were very settled. But Cecil wanted me to come back and run the Dennis Auto Plaza in south Kansas City, which included dealerships for Chevrolet, Mazda, Nissan, and Toyota. At that point I felt a bit like the fair-haired boy, winning dealer awards and building a strong reputation within the organization — I was confident and felt like I could do anything, even shifting gears so thoroughly and moving again after so long. Coming back home to be closer to my aging parents was an added draw that made sense to me at that time of our lives.

The Auto Plaza, however, had struggled and was leaking money like a sieve. It wasn't going to be an easy move. I knew I had a big challenge ahead, but my thorough, no-shortcuts philosophy had turned me into someone who could be called upon to help struggling locations. It took patience and hard work — work that followed a concrete but adaptable plan — and those above me in the organization had noticed it. It wasn't always flashy, but it was a reliable and successful approach.

I drove to Kansas City to be introduced on a Monday in January to 350 employees, knowing I would have the unenviable task of firing a significant number of people because the overhead was not commensurate with the size of the operation. Then the next day the United States entered the war against Iraq in Kuwait as part of Operation Desert Storm. Gas prices were sure to surge, and economic conditions would be uncertain for some time. There certainly weren't going to be any shortcuts to fixing this situation.

Paula and the girls, who had stayed in Decatur while I was getting settled and laying some groundwork at the Auto Plaza, moved about three months later. When their arrival day came, I figured they would be exhausted after a long day of being on the road, but I was just excited to see them after so long. As soon as they walked in the door, I went to hug them, but the girls instead went into rooms and started slamming doors.

"They're all yours!" Paula said. "They've been crying all the way from Decatur."

Another rough start. One that caught me a bit off-guard, though I probably should have expected it. The move back to Kansas City was, for me, a challenge but full of opportunity. It was much harder for the rest of my family to see anything other than what we were leaving behind. And I knew that my family deserved even greater levels of dedication and commitment than the dealership did.

And a year later those events and plans had come to fruition. The family had settled in and was embracing our new home city. The Auto Plaza was doing much better, and the dealerships in Decatur, of which I had retained ownership, were doing well under my appointed managers.

Then one day, totally out of the blue, Cecil called me and told me he had a deal to sell the Auto Plaza to another organization. I was floored. I had worked so hard to make this work for my family and my company, and now, in an instant, it was gone. I knew it was a business decision, and I respected that Cecil had to do what was in the best interest of his company, but it was still personally devastating.

In my early days as a manager, I had participated in an executive education program at the Wharton School of Business, but nothing I learned from a textbook or a lecture had prepared me for this. I didn't know what was going to happen next, but I knew I couldn't move my family again. Paula and the girls didn't want to move — not back to Decatur or anywhere else for that matter. I knew that if I was going somewhere else, I was going alone.

That long-term plan I had developed for myself that had been so beneficial and fruitful was going to need some serious tweaking. It was time to regroup, and I sat down and assessed my situation. The easy part of the decision concerned my family. I absolutely had to do what was best for them. They had made many sacrifices for my career, and it was at this juncture that I realized I needed a better and more consistent balance between my career and family. Not surprisingly, Cecil supported me on this as well and he stuck with me for the next two years — no shortcuts — while we looked for another situation that would suit both me and my family.

In the meantime, I still owned two dealerships in Decatur. I had turned them over to trusted managers and they continued to perform well, but it was necessary for me to check on them in person on a regular basis. For those two years I spent one week of every month in Decatur and the rest of the time back in Kansas City searching for another dealership to buy. I had a buddy named Dennis Spivak who owned a marketing company, and every morning he let me use his conference room to make calls to manufacturers and dealers to see what might be available in the region, with the aim of finding a new dealership to buy and getting back to work. It felt a little like the old days of calling up sales prospects and looking for new customers.

Finally, in October 1994, I found the deal I was looking for in Lawrence, Kansas, which is about 40 miles from Kansas City and the home of the University of Kansas. There was a Chevrolet and Oldsmobile dealership under the moniker of Sonny Hill Motors. The owner had several dealerships under the Sonny Hill umbrella, but he had filed for bankruptcy and was charged with falsifying his books to defraud lenders. In December of that same year, I was able to purchase a second Lawrence dealership, which was operated by an owner with struggling business interests abroad.

As one might conclude, these two organizations didn't have the best reputations, but I saw it as another opportunity to show what I could do and earn the trust of the community. As usual, the success of our stores would hinge on the people we hired, and after turning around several dealerships I had the confidence and the formula to do it again. But there was not going to be a short-term fix.

Two years and a lot of hard work later, a gentleman walked into one of our showrooms one day and asked to meet with our general manager, Dale Backs. He sat down and told Dale, "You all are doing business the right way around here, and we're going to support you." It turned out that endorsement carried significant weight. The business community had noticed our efforts and appreciated our determination not to cut the same corners the previous owners of these dealerships had.

My family was happy, the business was thriving, and my company had earned the respect of my new community. The years of setting goals, making plans, and adjusting with the circumstances were paying off.

Chapter 5
FACE WHAT YOU FEAR

Principle #5: Face your fears so
they can't hold you back

*In every situation, do the thing you fear. If you
do the thing you fear, the death of fear is certain.*
Ralph Waldo Emerson

I don't mind telling you that those early days for me as a car salesman, first at Clasen-Morse and then at Van Chevrolet, were full of anxiety and fear. My buddy Larry Spitcaufsky had thought I would do well as a salesman because, in his words, I had a personality that people could trust. When we were growing up, he kidded me that he and the rest of our group of friends kept me around because I was the one all the mothers loved and trusted, and my presence seemed enough to extend curfew.

While I was always outgoing and dealt well with people, selling automobiles was a whole different world. I had worked in a retail clothing store in my college days, but there was no comparison between convincing someone to buy a pair of pants and convincing them to buy a big-ticket item that cost thousands of dollars. Wheedling a few extra minutes out of a friend's mother and trying to persuade a stranger to spend hard-earned money are quite different prospects with very different stakes, and I knew that an outgoing and open personality alone would not be enough to save me in this business. For their part, the dealerships sent us to seminars, gave us training manuals, and taught us the basics of what to do. They taught us their "10 Steps to Success" and other proprietary processes and sales tactics. But to go out and face the public also required some personal hutzpah.

My first car sale at Clasen-Morse was to my parents. They bought a lime green 1971 Chevy Malibu Coupe, though they had declared for years that they would never buy a green car. But they enjoyed the ride and, now that their kids were all grown, they liked the idea of having a car that was sportier than an Impala.

Whatever their reasoning, it was a sale, and the staff initiated me in the tradition of cutting off my tie to celebrate my first one. Dealing with my parents, however, didn't help me much in overcoming the initial fears that came from approaching strangers and talking to them about the significant investment of a car purchase.

By the time I had made the move to Van Chevrolet and watched the veteran guys in action, I had begun to understand that there was a fear factor in the potential buyer's mind as well. When someone walked onto the showroom floor, they were likely just as nervous as I was. Back in the early 1970s, purchasing a car involved a much different process than today. With the internet, current-day buyers have a virtual cornucopia of information at their fingertips. They come into a dealership knowing generally what they want and what the likely cost is. In my early days in the industry, it wasn't like that at all. Car shoppers could hop from dealership to dealership to compare price, but they didn't have access to the kind of data that allowed them to make an informed purchase decision. Even with the amount of information buyers now have at their fingertips, car buying can still be nerve-wracking.

As I was growing up, my parents stressed the importance of sincerity and showing empathy, so that was always where I started when I wasn't sure how to proceed with a prospect. Once we shook hands and began getting to know each other, the relationship was able to start and in most cases the fear dissipated for both of us. The buyer and I developed a comfort level, a common ground. This helped me to view each customer, each person, as unique. Understanding that helped me tackle the fears and uncertainties of my customers and, as I grew more comfortable with my own process, conquer my own fears as well.

Logically, it seems silly to be fearful of seemingly routine encounters in our daily lives, but it's not uncommon to feel anxiety over a host of things that may seem trivial to those looking in from the outside. And there are so many comparatively bad events in the world that cause justifiable fear. While I was never in battle during my Army days, in my medical service I regularly saw what the horrors of war could do. Compared to such things it's impossible to justify the sort of fear that causes a person to be hesitant to talk to a stranger. We can tell ourselves there's nothing to cause us anxiety or worry in those small moments — it's not life and death, after all — but it's very hard to be convincing.

Let's face it — we all have innate fears and encounter circumstances which cause us anxiety. Some of these fears are very personal and unique to our own experiences and some are more commonly held. Some are quite rational and others less so. Even as they manifest in different ways, many of the fears that plague us, certainly all the ones that harried me as a young salesman, have common roots: fear of failure and fear of the unknown. And these can be very scary things indeed.

While fear and nervousness are normal and fairly common, these natural feelings to avoid disappointment, frustration, or regret by taking the safer path can still end up being counterproductive and at times even crippling. We hesitate when an opportunity comes by and miss the moment. At the heart of this hesitation is the fear of what unknown consequence will result if one fails. Am I going to look foolish? Am I going to disappoint a close friend or a loved one? Will my job or career be threatened if I make a mistake? These are all valid questions, and any action includes some risk.

I have had to overcome such fears on numerous occasions and not just with customers. That night in my parents' driveway when Paula thought I was uninterested in marriage and was ready to end our relationship, I had to make a quick but careful decision. In that case the choice was easy. Fear of an unknown but shared future with Paula was much less terrifying than the prospect of a life spent without the woman I loved. Not only did that decision result in decades of love and partnership, but it also spurred me to commit to a career that, at first, I wasn't too sure about. That fear I faced for Paula and the family we would make together.

Professionally, I have had more to cause me fear and anxiety than just awkward conversations with customers or failure to make a sale, difficult as that can be. When I was in Decatur, I was accused by the NCAA of providing vehicles as a prohibited benefit to basketball players at the University of Illinois. The allegations came from an assistant coach at Iowa, Bruce Pearl, who was, at that time, an assistant coach at Iowa and looking for ways to revenge himself for perceived slights related to recruiting. Even though his complaints had nothing to do with me and there was no substance to his accusations, I knew there could be an effect — potentially a very damaging one — on both my family and my business. I feared what it would do to the reputation I had worked so hard to establish over the years in the community and at work and what the future would hold if that happened.

Back in Kansas City in 1991, when I took over the Dennis Auto Plaza at the same time the United States military was invading Kuwait, there was great fear of a future filled with so many uncontrollable variables, a fear that was compounded when that dealership was sold the following year. My wife and daughters wouldn't be moving again, and I had no immediate prospects in the Kansas City area. I was scared that I could lose my family, and professionally I didn't know what I was going to do. I had trouble sleeping at night, as I asked God what he had in store for me. For two years I pursued every option I could think of, and it often seemed like nothing was going to work out no matter how hard I tried. The fear of failing in business and failing my family hovered over everything.

Fear itself is part of human nature and is not inherently bad, but it requires discernment. At its best it can keep us protected from real danger or physical pain, but it can be hard to distinguish between useful fear that produces caution and debilitating fear that paralyzes. Harmful fear needs clear-headed perspective to even it out. Without it, fear can take over the decision-making process and prevent us from capitalizing on opportunities that may require risk with potential for but not guarantee of returns.

Most situations that cause us fear and anxiety, however, are not so dramatic. They are moments when we must make small, brave choices or let opportunities pass us by. But these small moments add up and form patterns of expectation and behavior that will inform our decisions when the big moments come. Just as slowing down a sale and taking time to understand my customers' needs helped allay their fears in the moment, so slowing down and taking time to specifically understand the nature of one's own feelings of dread in a difficult situation can be instrumental in determining the best- and worst-case outcomes for potential pathways through. Being afraid of what others may think, or of failure to accomplish a designated task, is not the same as fear of catastrophic events. The stakes are not so high and even failure is not disastrous.

When we do make a mistake or have a failure, it can be easy to fall into the trap of thinking we're not qualified to ever get the job done, can't manage the situations we find ourselves in, and will certainly fail again. Then the next time there is a choice to make, we're afraid we'll make the wrong one, and so any decision at all can begin to feel impossible. This fear-based behavior pattern that makes it harder and harder to be decisive or feel confident in the choices made is even less likely to produce advantageous results and more likely to lead us to a fresh failure. It's a dark spiral that doesn't take long to form. As much as possible, I like to think of these as learning moments instead — opportunities to get better. I take the time to review my decisions and understand what I could have done differently to facilitate a more favorable outcome, and I stay focused on the potential for more failure but the potential for greater understanding and wisdom. As long as we don't make the same mistakes over and over again, we'll come out better.

The key to overcoming fear is to face it, to resist the paralysis of uncertainty and just do something to confront it. Often, any action at all, even an inexpert one, can help break the hold of fear and turn the unknown into something slightly more familiar. If there is hesitancy to talk to strangers, make an effort each day to introduce yourself to somebody new. Even if it never becomes fun to talk with strangers, at least you will know what to expect and come to understand your own best methods as you practice. If you get nervous on phone calls, then force yourself to make them until that fear subsides. Set a concrete goal for amounts and methods and, if necessary, find someone who will help keep you accountable to that goal. I promise it will happen. Fear won't necessarily disappear, but it will no longer be an impediment to accomplishing what needs to be done. No one is completely fearless, but no one ever reaches any measure of success or accomplishment without being able to act in spite of fear.

When I started in sales, one of the best ways I found of conquering my fears was to capitalize on each success and use it as a nudge forward. I recognized that I was at my best just after I'd sold a car, so if there was a prospect or cold call I needed to make, the best time to do it was right after a sale, because I was at my highest confidence level. It wasn't cockiness — it was a consistent self-assuredness — me as my best self — and it was apparent to everyone I encountered.

When facing the higher stakes of an NCAA investigation or the loss of a job, simple straightforward solutions or methods aren't as easy to come by (more on those situations later), but the bedrock remains the same. Hiding from the trouble — fearful paralysis — won't work and can even lead to new problems. And focusing only on failures in the past can blind us to the possibilities still ahead of us. As with most skills, the habits of small moments become the template for how we face the larger ones, in both good and bad ways.

As a business owner and entrepreneur, I make choices big and small on a constant basis, and I can't be hamstrung by the fear of mistakes or thinking that a wrong decision is going to ultimately lead to failure. Businessowners and entrepreneurs invariably make many, many mistakes, but successful businessowners and entrepreneurs learn and grow from them. Mistakes and adversity are a given in life and there is some comfort in that inevitability. No one can achieve perfection. And most of the time mistakes we make do not have calamitous outcomes. With the pressure of perfection and the threat of calamity both off the table, the missteps can seem less intimidating. It's not the mistakes themselves but how we react to them that will ultimately define our success, and no one who is afraid to take a calculated risk will ever be able reach the next level.

Another mitigator of fear, anxiety, and the accompanying stress is identifying what can be controlled and what can't. Concerning oneself with uncontrollable variables is a waste of time and only adds to an individual's stress level. A person's need to control everything is born both of fear and ego — fear of being wrong, fear of embarrassment or ridicule, and the foolish belief that any one human can have that much power. It is not productive to spend time fretting about what is beyond our control — things like the weather, other people's opinions, or in many cases events that have happened in the past — or wise to believe ourselves so venerably powerful. It is important that we have a plan to adjust to environmental factors based on what is under our control, and that we be canny enough to assess what power we do have.

Letting go of the desire for absolute control can help a person manage ego as well, which only enhances the possibility for success. People with overly large egos feel easily threatened and tend to lash out when faced with situations and people they can't control, and they often fear being discovered as inadequate by those who are capable and intelligent. They may fear they are going to be replaced or humiliated by those they view as rivals, even when those rivals are teammates. Big egos don't like to have their opinions challenged and blame others when events don't go the way they envisioned they should. This circle of inadequacy and blame prevents others from doing their best work and effectively prevents lasting success. In effect their fear of failure becomes a self-fulfilling prophesy.

I have seen this happen to others and make it a point to try to hire people smarter than I am, and I empower them to do their jobs with minimal interference from me. Since I already know that perfection is impossible, I don't have to have every skill myself or fear being supplanted by someone else. Just as Cecil gave me room to grow without being afraid of me, I am confident enough in my own set of capacities and skills to be able to appreciate and encourage what I see in others. We succeed better together as we complement each other.

I've always liked saying that I'm not smart enough to be scared. In reality, though, it's probably closer to the truth to say I'm not smart enough to have a long memory. At least not for failure and trouble. I have often been in positions to be fearful, moments when I worried for my reputation and felt that I had failed my family. But it has been the ability to continue looking forward through the fear, to see the unknown as an opportunity rather than a danger that gets me through. It puts me in the mode that if you have a plan and work it you can leave your fears behind. I work to accentuate the positive, to be a good person, and to work hard. And I keep my ego small enough to make sure that I always know that's enough.

Larry always said our lack of smarts was one of the things we had in common. In high school, he joked that we found our class rank on the floor. Maybe not the best method, but it was certainly early training for keeping our egos of a manageable size as we got older.

Coincidentally, or possibly not, Larry became a highly successful businessman.

Chapter 6
DO IT RIGHT AND SLEEP AT NIGHT

Principle #6: Lead your life the right
way and you'll have a clear conscience

*"Better is a quiet conscience than a prosperous
destiny. I prefer a good sleep to a good bed."*
Victor Hugo

I was taught by my parents and mentors that living a moral
life and respecting others is the only way to be a truly good
or happy person or to leave a worthy legacy. Character matters,
and your name and what you do with it matters. It shouldn't be
surprising then that my reputation is extremely important to
me, and I have always been determined to go to sleep each night
with a clear conscience, knowing that I've acted with integrity,
knowing that on that day I have done the best I could to please
God and serve other people. Obviously, we all have differences
of opinion with people — it's impossible to do business or even
interact with other people without occasional interpersonal
difficulties. In my own business, I'm sure there have been times

when customers have felt that they didn't get the best product or service at one of my dealerships. I have tried to minimize these instances over the years, however, and to always make every effort to make the relationship right.

In truth, a great deal of what creates a good reputation and enables clarity of conscience is wrapped up in how we approach relationships. Will we treat others fairly or selfishly? Will we be honest or use half-truths to serve our own agenda? Will we admit mistakes when we make them or blame others? How much do other people really matter? I had ample opportunity to reflect on all this and much more during my time in Decatur as I was swept up in the fallout of the actions of others who would have answered those questions very differently than I do.

I may never have managed top grades as a student, but I've always highly valued my time spent at college, the opportunities I found there, the formative time it was in my life. As I became more successful in business it was very natural for me to begin supporting the institutions of higher education that have been part of my background and of the communities where my businesses are located. Paula and I are longtime boosters of Pittsburg State, which is not only our alma mater, but also that of our daughter Mandi. Paula and I have been gratified to help with scholarships and many capital projects there over the years.

I also have a strong interest in sports and have loved basketball since my own playing days, and I enjoyed being in a position to support the programs at the universities near my dealerships over the years. In Decatur it was the University of Illinois, and since I've been in Lawrence, I've been a supporter of the University of Kansas.

Both Illinois and Kansas have traditions of producing highly ranked teams and NBA-quality talent, and it's been an honor to be associated with those programs and such great coaches as the late Lou Henson at Illinois and Bill Self at Kansas, both Hall of Famers. One of my biggest thrills was attending the 2008 Final Four in San Antonio when Kansas won the national championship. After the NCAA Tournament, Coach Self even did me the honor of allowing me to be part of the Jayhawks' championship team picture.

Over all these years, I'm proud that I have never done anything that has not been aboveboard, nothing that isn't in complete compliance with the rules of the NCAA, but when I was in Decatur my reputation came under fire anyway and seemed close to unraveling entirely.

In the spring of 1989, Illinois men's basketball was still basking in the glow of a spectacular season in which it posted a 31-5 record and reached its first Final Four in 37 years. Thanks to the leadership of the legendary Coach Henson and his great assistant coaches Jimmy Collins and Dick Nagy, it may have been the most talented team in school history. Nicknamed the Flyin' Illini, the team featured a bevy of athletic, NBA-caliber players who could play above the rim.

There were a number of car dealers in the state who participated in the school's Gifts-in-Kind program, offering the use of a complimentary auto to a coach or staff member in exchange for the right to purchase tickets for preferred seating at games — a common and accepted donation method used in most major collegiate athletic departments and allowed by the NCAA. I was pleased to participate in the program and to be able to provide a courtesy car for Nagy. Over the years, we became such good friends that I was invited to give the eulogy at his funeral in 2021.

Because of my friendships with the basketball coaches, I had earned their trust. They knew that I would make sure anyone they might refer to me for a car purchase, including any young college student unfamiliar with the sales and loan processes, would be treated well and given a fair deal. They also had complete faith that I would make sure everything was done properly, and there would be no special benefits provided in violation of NCAA rules.

In the summer of 1989, a few months after the Illini's Final Four appearance, I received a phone call from Steve Cameron, who at the time was the sports editor of the Decatur *Herald & Review*. We knew each other well, and he wanted to give me a heads up and get my take on a breaking story he'd learned about while covering a Chicago Cubs game at Wrigley Field. The Associated Press was reporting that Iowa assistant coach Bruce Pearl had contacted the NCAA about a car dealer in downstate Illinois who had allegedly given a Chevy Blazer and $80,000 to Deon Thomas, a high school senior being recruited by both Illinois and Iowa, so that he would sign a letter of intent to play basketball with the Illini.

"They wouldn't happen to be talking about you, would they?" Cameron asked me, referring to the car dealer involved in the report.

"No, of course not," I told him. "I have a relationship with Illinois, but I know better than to give away stuff to a recruit."

I felt certain then that this was some strange but easily explained mistake. I had never even contemplated such an egregious breach of ethics as bribing a recruit, nor had I been asked to do so by anyone at Illinois. I had treated people honestly, both personally and professionally, and followed the rules carefully — my name and reputation were at stake, after all. I was sure it would quickly become clear that there was nothing in the report or that it was about someone else and the whole thing would blow over.

Steve was sure that the report referred to me, however, and wanted to get ahead of the story and find out my response. I was a little taken aback, not only by the news but also by my feeling that trying to negate a report like that could backfire and make the situation look worse. But he thought I should say something, and he published a story with my denial.

As for the recruit himself, Deon Thomas had just graduated from Simeon High School in Chicago, where he was named "Mr. Basketball" for the state and a McDonald's All-American, and Iowa just had lost the recruiting battle for him. (Thomas would eventually go on to become the Illini's all-time leading scorer, a distinction he still holds.) Bruce Pearl, at the time a 29-year-old assistant coach and dogged recruiter, wasn't happy about Thomas choosing Illinois and had secretly recorded a phone conversation in which Thomas seemed to admit that Coach Collins at Illinois was arranging an offer of an SUV.

Soon more stories came out, and the NCAA started an investigation into Illinois that lasted 18 months. The claims about Thomas were quickly disproven. In interviews with the NCAA, Thomas steadfastly denied the allegations of misconduct, and said he was just saying anything to try to get rid of Pearl, who had taken to calling him several times a day. It's always been easy to sympathize with Thomas' predicament.

But the NCAA investigation opened everything up to scrutiny. I was the accused car dealer in the news story, and, because I had sold cars to current players, both the university and the NCAA started looking at those transactions. The attorney representing the university asked to see the associated paperwork. In my heart I knew I had behaved ethically and that I had nothing to hide. I gave the investigators and lawyers everything they asked for and more, anything that I thought might help show the truth of the matter and my desire to be open and honest.

Somewhere in all that, a new claim surfaced that players Steve Bardo, Nick Anderson, and Kendall Gill, all key contributors to the team's success, had received preferential treatment in obtaining car loans, but it was easy to show that wasn't the case. They had to come up with a five-to-10 percent down payment, just like every other customer, and qualify for financing through a bank the same as everyone else. Loan applications were processed through two local banks that handled financing for my two dealerships. The investigators wanted proof that I made a profit, and I shared the documentation that showed I earned a fair return on every deal. Though the NCAA determined there were some incomplete sections on the loan applications in question, even the banker who funded the loans said that wasn't unusual for any applicant.

Loren Tate, a highly respected local sports reporter who covered Illini athletics for decades and is a member of the U.S. Basketball Writers Hall of Fame, made an interesting observation in one of his columns at the time. Tate pointed out that all the transactions under investigation involved cars sold to Black players. No one questioned anything about one of the white players driving a new car, he wrote, and the assumption seemed to be that the Black players couldn't possibly afford even a used car, regardless of whether they had co-signing parents with good jobs or a strong future earning potential in the NBA. "It's as though a [B]lack student can't own a car," Gill was quoted in Tate's column, and it became easier and easier to see the inequity in the continued accusations on several fronts.

As for myself, I was devastated. I desperately wanted to prove myself innocent. Though I had followed all the rules, cut no corners, and treated people with fairness, still my integrity was being questioned. At our dealerships we were receiving anonymous phone calls at the switchboards from people accusing me personally of causing all these problems for Illinois and blaming me for the NCAA probe. My reputation in the community was being battered and it was hard to tell when or if it would ever be over.

In an effort to see the end of it, I even volunteered to have the NCAA investigators come in and interview me. They asked to do so without the presence of my attorney, but I wanted to be certain that everything was aboveboard and on the record, so they eventually agreed to allow him and a court reporter to be present.

By the end of 1990, a year and a half after that out-of-the-blue call from Steve Cameron, the NCAA Committee on Infractions had finally reached its conclusions. Though Illinois was found guilty of some violations, all were minor, and most were self-reported by the university during the course of the investigation, including the incomplete loan applications and the fact that Jimmy Collins had loaned Deon Thomas 10 bucks for a pizza (which he repaid the next day). Specifically with regard to me, however, the investigators seemed determined to remain suspicious of the loan applications and were unable to accept the assurances of honesty and appropriate dealings from players, coaches, banks, loan officers, or the many records they'd been provided. That final report read: "The committee found that three student-athletes in the basketball program purchased automobiles from a dealership operated by a representative of the university's athletics interests through special credit arrangements because of their status as university basketball players." I knew I hadn't done anything wrong. I had used standard, sound practices, and in the end, it was the bank, not me, who approved all the loans. But they couldn't go after the bank, so they went after me. It was infuriating.

Since the Illinois football team had previously been found guilty of violations under a since-fired coach in the 1980s, and because the investigations were only a few years apart, the university was cited for the proverbial "lack of institutional control," and the basketball program was hit with harsh sanctions. Among them were a reduction in scholarships, prohibitions on in-person recruiting, a ban from the 1991 NCAA Tournament, and a probation period of three years.

In addition, I was told to completely disassociate myself from the Illinois athletic department for that same three-year period, which didn't just mean that I couldn't participate in the courtesy car program — I couldn't even hold my usual season tickets. I received a lot of support from area sportswriters like Loren Tate, Steve Cameron, and Mark Tupper. They even noted that legal experts who had combed over the records of my transactions continued to be mystified by the NCAA ruling. The university also said they would appeal the sanctions against me, but nothing ever came of it.

I couldn't even attend games. I knew I could no longer have season tickets of my own, but on one occasion I'd been given tickets by a friend. While Paula and I were watching, however, the university attorney, who had spotted me in the stands, pulled me aside and told me I couldn't be there — I couldn't even stay and finish the game, I had to leave immediately. Paula and I left and went home. It felt like one of the last joys I still had from my time being connected to the basketball program had been taken away.

By this time, Cecil had already contacted me about returning to take over the Dennis Auto Plaza and I knew I was on my way back to Kansas City. As challenging as that circumstance came to be, the timing was probably good. Though I appreciated those who supported me in Decatur, damage had been done to my reputation that could not be easily undone. Tom McNamara, the sports editor at the *Decatur Tribune* who also worked part-time selling cars for me, was in my office once talking to me about the events with the Illinois basketball team, and I broke down. I'm an emotional guy who once cried for hours after we put down a pet Schnauzer named Schnitzel, and the thought that people would question my integrity, even more so in a highly public forum, was an overwhelming experience.

I had done all I could. I had been honest, both in my business dealings and with investigators. I had hoped to the last that this would be enough to exonerate me and my name within the community, but I was disappointed. Though I maintained a good relationship with the basketball coaches, particularly Dick Nagy, I was disappointed that I didn't receive more support from the athletic department.

One final note on this whole sad affair — in 2012, Mark Tupper reported that during that year's Final Four weekend in New Orleans, Bruce Pearl crossed paths with Jimmy Collins. Coach Collins had recently retired from his own head coaching position, and Pearl was waiting out a three-year show-cause penalty after being fired at Tennessee for NCAA violations. The two men passed each other on the street without saying a word, but then Pearl turned around and walked back. He extended his hand to Collins and offered an apology for the misery he unleashed at Illinois. "I'm sorry, Jimmy," Pearl said, according to an eyewitness who contacted Tupper with the report. "I was young. I was stupid. I was immature. Deon was the victim." According to another report in *The Athletic*, Pearl also made peace with Deon Thomas that same weekend.

If Pearl ever considered the damage he did to me, my family, or my reputation, it seems never to have troubled him enough to add me to the list of people he should make peace with.

Many years have gone by since that unpleasant episode in my life. I've had other adversities, of course, but having my reputation unfairly sullied was among the most painful events I've ever endured, particularly when the origin of it was so highly visible. I have retained a thick file in my records that I labeled "NCAA Bullshit," which contains transcripts of the attorney interviews, copies of letters I received during that time period — both good and bad — and numerous newspapers stories and columns related to the investigation.

I don't look at it often, but I like to keep it around as a reminder that sometimes even our best efforts, even efforts backed by truth and integrity, are sometimes not enough to overcome the effects of people with agendas designed to cause harm. But this makes it all the more necessary for me to work daily to keep my conscience clear in the way I handle my business and the people around me. Only that will ensure that you still have the people who know and love you on your side to support you when others fail you.

• • • •

The keys to a clear conscience are quite simple, rooted in ethical and moral behavior. In our daily lives we need honesty, compassion, and the acceptance of personal responsibility, especially when confronted with life's challenges. These values translate well to our business practices, too. Values-based behaviors can influence how an entire organization operates, but it's even more incumbent on those in ownership or management positions to have high ethical standards. This sets a tone for the organization that will dictate how the customers are served and the employees are treated. Ethics and morals in business mandate transparency, development of trust, accountability, and respect among all associates. There must be complete honesty and clear communication, which build trust throughout the team, with the customers, and in the community.

We don't need to look far for examples of companies that lost their moral compass and violated the public's trust. A common thread in all of them is that greed obliterated conscience, and now we know their names for all the wrong reasons. Enron used fraudulent accounting practices to appear profitable while actually suffering substantial losses, went bankrupt, and was liquidated. Auditing firm Arthur Andersen, also implicated in the Enron scandal, surrendered its licenses to practice, virtually ending its viability as one of the nation's largest accounting firms after more than 90 years in business. Lehman Brothers, Worldcom, Uber, Theranos. We know their scandals and their sins — reputations ruined and lives destroyed for lack of a stable set of guiding values.

Failures like these put more of a premium on honest and ethical business practices and can provide a unique opportunity for entrepreneurs who have earned the trust of their constituents. The corporate giants and big box stores may be able to offer lower prices, but seldom garner the trust of a jaded public the way a community-conscious, local businessperson can.

Closer to home for me was the 2015 scandal involving Volkswagen, a name affixed to one of my Lawrence dealerships. VW was found to have intentionally programmed their "clean diesel" engines to activate their emissions controls only during lab testing, so that their cars would appear to be in compliance with EPA standards while not actually being so. Hundreds of thousands of cars sold in the U.S. were affected, and when the case settled, customers were given the choice of a buyback or a free fix plus compensation.

The timing of that situation was particularly difficult for me — another example of the actions of others impacting my own reputation in the community. Not long before the story broke, I was invited to a regional meeting in Houston by Volkswagen with their top executives, including Michael Horn, who was the CEO of the Volkswagen Group of America. They indicated a desire to expand certain markets, and we discussed the possibility of a VW dealership in Kansas.

After our meeting I had a side session with the regional manager out of Dallas, and I told him I was interested in future expansion, including under their Audi brand. I got all excited, flew back home on a Thursday and got up Friday morning fired up and ready to go to work. I was thinking that business was good, VW loved me, and I had the new possibility of even expanding to an Audi dealership.

On the drive in, however, the news on the radio informed me that Volkswagen was being investigated for deceptive practices in their emissions reporting. My heart stopped. Forget expansion, how would my current dealership be able to navigate through this mess?

I had already told my general manager at the Volkswagen dealership what a great day we'd had in Dallas, and now it was all jeopardized. According to a 2020 VW assessment, the scandal had cost them about $35 billion worldwide in fines and settlements, and in the United States Michael Horn stepped aside from his CEO position. We had been selling 50 to 60 of their cars a month, and, since about 40 percent of those were diesel, it dropped to 30 to 35. Those numbers were a gut punch, and I had to scramble to find ways to make up the difference.

It all could have been avoided, too, by simple honesty at almost any stage of the process. They could have been up-front about the actual capability of their engines or spent more money or time on research and development to engineer what they needed to make their clean air goals a reality. Even when the issue was originally discovered by a University of West Virginia professor and three students who were doing emissions testing for a research project, the professor initially contacted the company to discuss his findings. But instead of taking the issue seriously or looking for ways to resolve it, VW basically blew him off, so the research team took their findings to the EPA instead.

Financially we made it through. For all their mistakes, Volkswagen did pay out in the end to make things as right as they could be. We were paid for the devaluation of the franchise, and for a while we also were receiving additional money each month to subsidize repair costs. But the damage had been done to the good name we had worked so hard to build at Crown Volkswagen. We told customers that VW would take care of them, which they did, yet some were still irate and blamed us on a local level when they needed someone to shout at.

With a clear conscience, I know that I can stand tall and fight when there is difficulty. Then, whatever the outcome, either good or painful, I know at least that I need not be ashamed of myself or my conduct, that I have not failed those who love me, or done business in ways that are selfish and have hurt the innocent or the trusting. Even a genuine error in judgement need not be multiplied by hiding it or blaming others. I don't need to fear the consequences of a single mistake any more than I need to define myself by it. We make it right, we learn, we move forward.

Because missteps and challenges along the way are inevitable in business, not everybody is going to believe their situation has been handled fairly. In today's world anybody can post anything on the internet, and people can always threaten a lawsuit claiming they were mistreated. Reputations are more fragile than ever. In a competitive industry such as the automotive business, you're going to get questioned. But I have found when we stick to our scruples and processes, we do fine in the balance.

When there are problems, though, be transparent. Provide employees, customers, suppliers, and the public as much information as possible without breaching the boundaries of confidentiality, even if it's bad news. That was one of my great frustrations when Steve Cameron called me about the Illinois situation: I didn't have time to manage or expand the information before someone else's incorrect version became public. It may not always be possible, but when it is, get out in front of the message. This isn't simply about "damage control"; rather it's about taking the early opportunity to fix or minimize damage before it has a chance to rage out of control and harm innocent people.

At the root of my core values is that I believe in what I'm doing. I get up every morning and get to work on helping my family and making my business better. And when I go to sleep at night, I know I've done what I set out to do when the day began in the best possible manner, so I keep my vision focused forward instead of looking backward. I know I have been fair with people, I have been honest, and I have made the members of my team contributors to the success of the business.

• • • •

In the end, a clear conscience is one of those few intangibles that we take to our grave. Dick Nagy reinforced that for me in my final days in Illinois, when he wrote a letter to the editor of the local paper about the situation and "the first stern test of our relationship" after the conclusion of the investigation.

"Now that many of the difficulties have become the data for reconstruction by historians," he wrote, "I marvel at what remains. Our friendship is stronger now than before. Through all the confusion and finger-pointing, we each put the other first. Defense was unnecessary since no wrongdoing occurred, but each one of us provided a foundation for the other. My, oh my, what friendship can do."

LORD OF THE RINGS

The Gifts-in-Kind program at the University of Illinois held a lot of appeal for me when I had my dealerships in Decatur. It was a chance to help support the program, and through it I developed a special friendship with Dick Nagy. I also had good relationships with Head Coach Lou Henson and Assistant Coach Jimmy Collins, and they would let me tag along on some road trips. I even got to sit behind and even sometimes at the end of the players' bench, which I really enjoyed.

In 1984, the Illini shared the Big Ten Championship with Purdue. It was the first time they had won or shared a conference title in 21 years, and they wouldn't do it again until 1998. It was an epic season highlighted by four overtime wins, including a victory over Michigan that went into four extra periods. The campaign ended in a heartbreaking 54-51 Elite Eight loss to Kentucky that was played in Lexington on the Wildcats' home floor. There was a lot of controversy surrounding that game, and partly as a result it was the last NCAA tournament in which a team was allowed to host a regional game in its own arena.

As is customary, the players, coaches, and support staff received championship rings. Coach Nagy wanted to buy me a championship ring in recognition of my contributions, but Coach Henson didn't think that was proper since I wasn't a direct participant in the basketball program. Now anyone who knew Dick understood how persistent he could be, and he kept the pressure on his boss, citing my support of the program even through some difficult times. Lou finally acquiesced, and I received that ring. I found out later that Dick paid for it out of his own pocket.

It was a great honor, and I wore the ring proudly long after I left Decatur. When I moved to Lawrence, I became an equally ardent booster of the Kansas basketball team. I had not grown up as a Kansas fan, and in fact during my early years of college I spent most of my weekends at the University of Missouri partying with some of my old high school buddies. But now that I was in Lawrence, it was good business to root for the Jayhawks, and with their rich basketball tradition it wasn't too hard to become interested and involved, especially with my love for the game.

When I arrived in Lawrence in 1994, the head coach was Roy Williams, who had a great deal of success, but in 2003 he left to take the job at his alma mater, North Carolina. He was succeeded by Bill Self, who came to KU from, coincidentally, Illinois. The first time I met Bill we shook hands, and he spotted my Illinois championship ring. He looked me straight in the eye and said, "I'm going to replace that for you." He joked one time with a newspaper reporter that he didn't appreciate me wearing that ring, and he was determined to get me a new one with the Jayhawk logo.

And did he ever live up to his word! In 2008, Kansas won a dramatic overtime game against Memphis to claim its first NCAA Championship in 20 years, and I was in San Antonio to witness it. When it came time to issue the rings the team included me on the list of recipients. What an honor that was!

Kansas consistently won the Big 12 championship, and Coach Self included me on the recipients of the conference championship rings. Between 2005 and 2018 the Jayhawks won or shared 14 consecutive Big 12 Conference championships, an unprecedented feat, and they had a special commemorative ring issued to celebrate the achievement. It's been a privilege to be associated with his program, and another reason I am proud to have helped him start his Assists Foundation, which has raised millions of dollars to support youth sports.

I also received a championship ring when my alma mater, Pittsburg State, won the 2011 NCAA Division II national championship in football. I'll wear that one occasionally, too, because I'm so proud of the accomplishments of that athletic department and of how big a role that school has played in my family's life.

I still keep that Illinois ring in a special place among my trove of memorabilia, and for the right occasion I'll put it on again. In 2015, Lou Henson was inducted into the College Basketball Hall of Fame, which happens to be located in Kansas City. Dick Nagy also attended, and I made sure to say hello to both him and Lou and show them the ring. I shared a laugh with Dick when I reminded him how persistent he was in getting me the ring those many years ago. Both of those men have since left us; Lou passed away in 2020 at the age of 88, and Dick died in 2021 at 78. In giving Dick's eulogy, I was able to share the story of the ring — and a smile — one more time.

I've been lucky to be so appreciated by and participate behind the scenes with three championship athletic programs. They've left me memories, and rings, that have lasted a lifetime.

Chapter 7
EVERYONE'S A PROSPECT

Principle #7: Treat all people with dignity

*"Do right. Do your best. Treat others
as you want to be treated."*
Lou Holtz

When **I** think back about the lessons I learned from my parents, the trait that stands out above all is kindness. There are some who think kindness is a sign of weakness, that "kind" should be viewed as a four-letter word synonymous with a lack of toughness. But Mom and Dad taught me that it is a strength. In fact, the impact of showing kindness has done more to bring me respect than anything else. Ironically perhaps, it's also how I try to show respect to others.

When I first meet someone, it is my intent to make them feel at ease, to comfort them if they seem to be in need, and to extend a helping hand whenever I can. I try not to begin with any supposition that I am better than they are or that they are better than I am. I like to think I am also pretty good at reading people — a skill honed after many decades in sales — but I start with the assumption that people are trustworthy. It's not difficult to be friendly and extend a simple pleasant greeting or warm handshake.

Treating people with respect and dignity is valuable in its own right and for its own sake, but it is also a sound business practice. Whenever I go out to eat, I make a habit of giving a generous tip and leaving my business card with the ticket. You never know when you might be meeting your next customer or a prospect for future employment. That server may be in the market for a car soon, or they may be thinking about possibilities for a new career that I might be able to give them.

Not long ago I was having dinner with Larry, and we had an exceptional server. She was polite, attentive, and had an engaging personality. I gave her my business card and told her that if she ever wanted to get in another line of business we had multiple opportunities — not just in sales but in business development, human resources, and customer relations as well. A short time later I received from her a very nice handwritten note letting me know that she appreciated our conversation and thanking me for the introduction to a potential new opportunity. She said that if I ever came back in the restaurant to ask for her to be the server and she'd take care of me. I haven't given up the hope that I might still be able to hire her myself someday, but until then I know one restaurant in town where I'll be getting great service. Even if she never joins our team, I promise you she'll think of Crown Automotive the next time she's in the market for a new car.

Our dealership also contracts out with a small business that employs a few people to wash cars, and they'll get the vehicles clean and ready when we're preparing to deliver them to the buyers. This saves us money rather than employing full-time people on our own, in addition to supporting a local small business. Normally the car washers are young folks just starting out or trying to make a few extra bucks for school, and I'll sometimes go through that area when they're working and hand each one a $100 bill as a little bonus to show my appreciation. They do good work and have certainly earned this occasional incentive.

You should see the looks on their faces. It's neither expected nor anticipated by them, but it probably makes me feel even better than it does them. They thank me profusely, and every time I see them again they go out of their way to ask me if they can wash my car or do anything else for me.

I especially like to reward people for effort that's given when they think they're not being watched or monitored. I like to say that I have a knack for being in the right place at the wrong time, or maybe it's the wrong place at the right time. Either way, what I see when people don't think I'm present or observant is very telling. If someone is dogging it and not doing their best work when the manager is out of sight, they may need some counseling from their supervisor. But much more frequently I witness the opposite — people doing a good job without supervision — and it's then that I want to provide tangible evidence of my appreciation. I share a little kindness out of my own surplus, and suddenly I have that many more people moving around, eager to spread around their own efforts and good attitude wherever they go.

This might sound like common sense, but my continual goal is to show every person I meet the proper respect and dignity that every human being deserves. They may end up disappointing me at some point — some always will, just as there are those I'm sure I sometimes disappoint — but I want to give them a chance to be seen as they wish to be seen. I would rather occasionally suffer the disappointment of trusting too much than be hardhearted and cynical when I look at the world around me. I've had a lot of unexpected people in my life do nice things for me, and it feels like it is incumbent upon me to "pay it forward."

We hear that expression a lot, and in fact it has been overused to the point where it tends to lose its impact, but we all know the concept. It simply means that if something good happens to a person they turn around and do something good for someone else. Instead of paying back a good deed, you turn around and do a new good deed for someone else in your sphere. It has a lot in common with the ideas of karma and the Golden Rule, and I'm a big believer in spreading our own good fortune out to those around us, be they friends and neighbors, customers, or complete strangers.

And, while having money and resources can certainly be helpful, wealth is not a prerequisite to paying it forward. It can look like a big tip left for an overworked server in a restaurant, but it can just as easily take the form of seeing and showing care to one who is overlooked, taking the time to help someone with a difficult task, or listening to the voice of those who are often silenced. Going that extra mile, or in many cases just an extra few inches, can make all the difference in the world to someone in need.

When we are able to use material resources, we needn't make the mistake of thinking it's only big amounts that make a difference. It can be as simple as buying a stranger's beverage at your local coffee shop, and I've seen the result of that unexpected kindness on the faces of those who receive it. When we live in a way that spreads kindness and human dignity forward, we may be affecting someone's situation in ways we can't begin to comprehend and will never know about. Small acts have the power to change a person's outlook, attitude, even their actions as they continue on and hopefully spread kindness forward even further.

Since I have been given much, however, I try always to be looking for opportunities to help people in ways they couldn't help themselves. I know what it is in my own life to be grateful to those who have gone above and beyond to help me. Though it feels great to see the smiles when someone receives the gift of a free spirit-lifting latte, I also know I can do more.

One time when I was in Florida, I was stopped at a street corner where a young man was asking for money. He didn't look like your stereotypical panhandler, and something about him caught my attention. When I pulled up to the intersection, we were almost face-to-face, and instead of avoiding eye contact or just driving on by, I asked him what he was doing and why. He said he'd had some problems within his family and needed to move on, that he wanted to make something of himself and needed a few bucks to get started, but also that he was embarrassed to be out there begging. I gave him 10 cents worth of businessman's advice and 20 actual dollars to maybe help him on his way. It was a small interaction and it's possible that he was lying, but I don't think he was. I hope I helped lift his spirits, that he could tell I saw him as a person and not just a nameless panhandler, and that I contributed in a small way to him being able to find a way to live a good life.

Helping people find ways to live a good life has been a big point of emphasis in much of my philanthropic work. I have long had a heart for and been privileged to support organizations that serve people with disabilities, who also deserve to be treated with proper respect and dignity but often aren't. For many years,

I have served on the Board of Trustees for Cottonwood, Inc., a not-for-profit organization in Lawrence helping individuals with disabilities develop vocational skills for job placement. It's been one of the most satisfying associations I've had in my life as I've witnessed the achievements of their clients.

One Cottonwood friend I've known for a long time is Cole Browne. Cole was diagnosed at an early age with cerebral palsy that resulted in some developmental disabilities, but he has thrived as a client of Cottonwood's. Now 39 years old, Cole is an independent man who owns his own home and has a good job at Chili's, where he makes great use of his social skills and receives many compliments from customers on his professionalism. I'm proud to be part of the organization that has helped him create a good life for himself.

• • • •

Most people will be in the market for a car at some point in their life. A chance encounter highlighted by a good deed might provide the impetus for a person to remember my dealerships if and when the need for an automobile arises. And this is the case for most types of businesses. Very few are so specialized that kindness in the community wouldn't help expand the number of reachable customers.

While that's true, there is one caveat — everyone may be a prospect, but not everyone will ultimately turn out to be a customer, and that's okay. We can't expect every act of kindness or respect to end in a business deal, and not every relationship needs to or should be mined for its business potential. As much as I want to sell a car to everyone, it's not going to happen. I learned this many years ago when I was in Decatur, and as usual Paula was the one who imparted the wisdom.

Back then I was a young dealer, and my goals were to make everyone happy and have everyone I knew buy all their cars from me. At the time I was also on the board of the local YMCA, and at one of our meetings a fellow board member sitting next to me was waxing on about how much he enjoyed the new Buick he had just purchased. He told me all about what a great car it was and about its many features. Excited about his new vehicle, he didn't see how personally I was taking it.

I looked him straight in the eye and said, "I really appreciate that you love your new car, but I sell Oldsmobile, Chevrolet, Nissan, and Toyota." I swear at the time I thought I was trying to be nice about it, but I basically told him that I couldn't care less about his Buick and that since we were on the same board he should have bought his car from me.

After the meeting I went home and told Paula, "Can you believe that guy bought a Buick when he knows I'm an Oldsmobile dealer?" The similarity of the two makes of cars made his choice seem even more galling.

"Not everyone you know is going to want to buy a car from you," she answered. "They may not want you to know everything about them when they fill out a credit application. Maybe their credit isn't great, or maybe they don't want you to know how much they make. Maybe they have another friend on a different car lot. Maybe they just like Buicks."

Lesson learned. It's good and natural to want people we know to become customers so we can treat them well and share our expertise with them, but we also must respect others enough to allow for choices we may not always understand or even like. Your friends are your friends, even when they're not also your customers.

Too many people are caught up in themselves and wanting to know "what's in it for me" — as even I was somewhat guilty of in that moment — instead of understanding the true reward you receive by doing something good for somebody else. The saying goes that the more you give the more you get, and the more you get the more you give. I believe that's true and have tried to live that way.

Adhering to a principle of treating everyone with dignity and respect has provided me untold benefits — some tangible but mostly intangible. I make an effort to be sensitive to everyone's needs, to provide proper validation to a friend or a stranger for a job well done, to provide a hand up for someone struggling to survive. When we treat people properly, we discover not only the best version of others, but also of ourselves.

Chapter 8

TUNE UP YOUR RELATIONSHIPS

Principle #8: Work to build rapport with coworkers, customers, friends, and family

> *"Building and repairing relationships are long-term investments."*
>
> Stephen Covey

When we climb that ladder of achievement, we pass a lot of people on the way up, and if we're lucky we might get to the top. Reaching that pinnacle may be the ultimate goal, but a lot of people end up finding out that it can be lonely up there. The higher you get on that ladder the more isolated you may feel, and the fewer trusted relationships you may have. There are lots of reasons for this, many of them a result of our own suspect choices. In our haste to achieve, we may have gotten too busy and cut off our contacts or even neglected the people who mean the most to us. Or we may never have taken the time to build those relationships in the first place.

When fortunes change, as they often do, businesses may fail, marriages may end in divorce, and relationships may crumble. If you've been intentional about building and maintaining relationships, however, then one or more of those people whom you treated well on the way up will help keep you from hitting the bottom on the way back down.

Through the years, I have tried to work on building relationships with my co-workers, community, and my family. I haven't always been as successful at it as I would like and have had to make course corrections along the way, but I'm fortunate that I've always had people who cared enough about me and our relationship that they were willing to be truthful with me and help me get back on track.

Professionally, I've had a lot of success over the years, but I've also had enough failures and setbacks to keep me realistic about how quickly things can change. In the good times and bad, it's been a blessing to me to have the built those relationships so that I have the support of not only my family members and business associates, but also the trust and confidence of people throughout the communities in which I've worked and lived. It's these relationships, not our pursuit of goals or subjective success, that must always provide the bedrock of our lives and even of our careers and businesses.

In building a business, I work to surround myself with others who share my goals and my passions. In turn I want to get to know them and find out what makes them tick, so that they feel valued and appreciated. I make it a practice to regularly recognize achievements of individuals on my team as one practical way of making sure they feel seen. Creating good, long-lasting working relationships begins with knowing my team members as individuals and to make sure there are strong and stable lines of communication, so they know their voices are heard and that I do, in fact, care about who they are and what they think.

One of the early steps I took as a new businessowner was the creation of a group called the Employee Involvement Committee, which was designed to keep the staff apprised of happenings in the company and to include our people in some of the decision-making processes — tangible ways of being seen and heard and forming healthy working relationships. One person from each department who was not a manager would form this committee which would then meet with me on a periodic basis. Their job was to bring suggestions from their individual department meetings on ways we could improve as a company. I tasked them to look beyond typical things like "we should get raises" or any personal issues affecting individuals in their group. I wanted them to be creatively engaged to bring new ideas to improve our working environment, our brand, and our customer service. If a proposal made sense and could be implemented at a fair cost, we'd pursue it further. And if I had to table a suggestion to consider it further, I pledged that no matter what the answer was I'd get back to them with a decision in a timely manner.

Recommendations ranged from providing an opportunity for employees to obtain cancer insurance to improvements in the building's landscaping to giving the Employee of the Month a special parking place. We also reviewed what charities and philanthropic organizations we would support, which has always been central to my being, and it was great being able to be part of helping the team find new passions, take more ownership of their roles in our organization, and grow in relationship to each other and to me.

Many businessowners make the mistake of focusing too heavily on the revenue side and overemphasizing the contributions of the sales or service staff, to the detriment of other team members who are making significant contributions to the organization. With this committee the entire staff had the chance to provide input for the good of the company, so that every member of every department felt like they could make a difference. From the owner to the managers to the support staff to the clean-up crew, all were empowered to find ways to fix problems or offer advice for improvement.

In fact, our biggest problem was just finding a time for everyone to meet. The technicians in the service area don't work the same hours as the salespeople on the showroom floor, their schedules don't coincide with the office staff, and lunch breaks never match up. In some setups, I found the scheduling difficulties rendered it impractical, but employee engagement and input remain of paramount importance to me, so we find new ways and methods to make it work. I want employees to know that there are processes for them to be involved in decision-making and offering new ideas, so I now have a larger human resources staff, plus a full-time customer relations manager and philanthropic manager, and the structure is in place for suggestions to run through them. We continue to have department meetings on a regular basis, and the managers are encouraged to bring me feedback from their respective staffs. I make it clear that I want to hear people's voices and that those voices matter.

Building relationships also extends to our clientele. I love to see repeat customers and am thrilled when they bring their own friends and family members to us, expanding our customer community. There is no greater compliment in business than a customer referral. However, in my five decades in the car business, I've learned that not every customer is going to be satisfied, and some are going to complain no matter what. It's just human nature. But that does not preclude me from making the effort to establish a workable relationship with them, and I have found that by doing so I can often defuse a potential confrontation. That relationship may be a one-time encounter, but if you take the time to talk to someone you can usually learn enough to find out what their real need is and give them the proper attention.

It's my philosophy not to allow tense moments to grow into full-blown conflagrations. Nobody wins in those situations. My general manager Dale Backs was the best at settling people down. He'd bring them into the office and tell them to just talk facts. They could scream and holler all they wanted, but in his patient way he showed them that it didn't accomplish anything. Maybe they'd had a bad day at home, or their spouse had made them mad, or work had been rough, or maybe just the stress of a car with a problem had driven them crazy. So Dale would go into a calm dissertation in his office focused on facts instead of emotions, and by the time the customer exited his office Dale would have his arm around them and they'd be hugging.

I never quite had Dale's talent, but I had plenty of opportunities to practice the art of fostering functional relationships with angry people. I remember from my days as the general manager at Van Chevrolet a customer who was on our service drive raising hell — screaming and hollering about his Monte Carlo. Usually, the service managers are able to handle these instances by themselves and prefer I stay in my office, because if the owner comes out that sometimes makes the customer even more demonstrative. But in this case, it was obvious that my only choice was to get involved.

It turned out that the steering column on the Monte Carlo had gotten cockeyed and wasn't straight, and this gentleman had gone into a meltdown complaining about it. I tried to appease him, but I wasn't making a lot of progress.

"This car's a piece of shit," he said, and then followed it up with a line I'll never forget. "I think I'm just going to drive this car up your butt!"

While I was plenty irritated at that point, I had to stifle a chuckle at that remark. "There isn't any room in there," I told him. "There's already two other cars taking up space."

His over-the-top reaction pegged him as an attention-seeking kind of person, though, and he was unlikely to stop with his antics until he received immediate satisfaction. We already had a full bay of cars being worked on in the service area, so I couldn't just pull one of them out to get his repair done. I knew I would have to get creative to appease him and bring this situation to a conclusion.

"Buddy," I told him, "I don't have room to pull your car in there right now, so I'm going to have someone come out and fix it right here on the drive, and we'll get you on your way as soon as possible."

Fixing a car right on the drive was not a normal nor an easy procedure. But my offer worked to settle him down. I had found a connection and calmed the storm. And I felt relieved that he wasn't going to go through with his threat to drive the car up my butt. We got his problem fixed right there and, as I promised, he was on his way.

We later found out that this guy actually worked on the assembly line at a General Motors plant where they installed the steering columns for this exact Monte Carlo model. So he was screaming about the component that he had helped assemble on that very car! He forgot to mention that during our conversation.

I had another customer in Decatur who had bought a Chevrolet truck and the paint was peeling off. He was about 6-foot-4, 350 pounds, and becoming more irate by the minute about the paint and what a bad vehicle it was. I stopped him and said, "Let me just buy this truck back from you. We can trade it out for another one or I'll just give you your money back." It's a suggestion I've made more than once when someone has crossed the line into pure emotion and illogic. No reasonable compromise is likely to reach them in that state, and I figure life's too short to spend it shouting and being shouted at over a car.

I've never had anyone take me up on it, though, and this guy was no exception. The thought of entirely giving up the vehicle suddenly brought him back to earth. He calmed down and said he loved the truck, but understandably didn't like the way the paint was peeling. He wanted me to repaint it, to which I readily agreed, and we made him happy. After that, his disposition was as soft as butter in your hands, and we became buddies. It was a miraculous change in his attitude. Which, considering his size, I was happy about.

Most of the time, people just want to know you care. They want to be heard and know that as the businessowner I am really trying to take care of them.

• • • •

One of the toughest people for me to develop a relationship with, personally or professionally, was Cecil Van Tuyl. For a guy whose stated personal philosophy was all about people, he really didn't have a lot of time for you until you had proven yourself on his terms. He worked nonstop, and he was always looking for the next potential partner or business opportunity. Once I had shown that I could be a significant contributor to his organization, however, he became a mentor and eventually a business partner. Though he was a tough nut to crack, doing so was well worth the effort. Professionally, the mentoring and support I received from him were invaluable and formed the foundation for everything that I've been able to build these last several decades. Personally, the confidence his support gave me in difficult times helped those times pass. He was one of the mentors who helped keep me from hitting the bottom.

I'm more hands-on than he was, in part because my dealerships pale in size compared to the business empire that he built. I'm able to know all my employees in ways he simply couldn't. But he did teach me a lesson about the entwinement of relationships within an organization. When I hire a new salesperson today, I always ask them why they want to be in the car business. Then I follow that with my usual speech about making this a career and not just a job, and that the harder you work the luckier you get — it may sound a bit cliché to a new person coming in, but I hope they can tell I'm sincere.

I also make it a point to tell them that the more success they have, the better we'll get to know each other. And the better we get to know each other, the more success they'll have. They come to understand quickly that we work best and most effectively if we genuinely care about each other as players on the same team. When they're successful, they're not only making a living for themselves but also for me, their managers, and everyone else within the organization. By selling more cars they create more opportunities in the service and parts departments, the dealership grows, more jobs are created, and we all prosper. But if their effort falls short and they don't contribute their fair share, they're going to have a tough time building solid relationships or finding much success within the organization.

The most important relationships I have built, however, have been my own friends and family — the support system I have around me, giving me strength and joy daily. And as anyone who's ever had a friend or family member can tell you, these are often the most difficult relationships to shape.

It helps to have a great life partner, as I have had with Paula, who keeps me focused and grounded and is always there to offer a sound perspective when we're making family decisions. She has also not hesitated to let me know when business priorities must be secondary to those of the family, as happened after we moved back from Decatur in the early '90s.

And I couldn't be prouder of my two daughters. They have grown up to be incredible women — each unique and successful in their own ways. However, as anyone who has ever raised a child knows, kids present challenges as they mature, and despite my best efforts to build our relationships, there were bumps along the way.

Everybody has always told Mandi she looks like me, and we have some of the same personality traits — both emotional and sensitive people. And Mandi went to Pittsburg State and initially struggled academically (just like dear old Dad did), but she managed in the end, graduated with a degree in Elementary Education, then earned her master's at Baker University in fitness and nutrition. While she was at Pitt State, she entered into a relationship which resulted in a short-lived marriage, but also gave me my only grandchild, Maddox, who's one of the lights of my life. He has become a wonderful young man and, while Mandi has instilled in him excellent study habits, he also loves to play basketball for his high school and his AAU teams. It is an absolute joy to watch him grow and compete.

When Mandi was going through the divorce with a 6-month-old baby, Paula and I were continually amazed by our daughter as she grew and matured in the midst of that difficult situation. As we have watched her ably handle the joys and trials of single motherhood, my relationship with and admiration for her have deepened. Probably the greatest compliment she could have given me was when she told me once that I'm a role model for her, and when she has a decision to make, she often asks herself, "What would Miles do?"

Our younger daughter, Ali, was an athlete, band member, and an honor student in high school, and then headed to Boston University, deciding to stretch her fledgling wings. I happened to be passing through the kitchen while Paula was on the phone with her one day during her freshman year, and she stopped me to say, "Ali wants to talk with you."

I took the phone to hear my daughter say, "How ya doing? Mom probably wanted me to tell you that I had a nose piercing with a ring inserted."

"Why?" I asked. Images of my daughter with a massive gold fortune-teller's hoop poking off the front of her face ran rampant through my mind.

She went into a discourse that sounded a bit rehearsed about being independent and doing things on her own, to which I replied, with great finality, "Ali, take it out. You can't have a ring in your nose."

I then launched into my sales pitch mode and told her that employers wouldn't want to hire her with a ring in her nose. When she was trying to interview or talk during a meeting or give a sales pitch, people would be focused on her nose and not what she was saying. She became emotional, upset and frustrated by my response to her small act of autonomy, and I paused just long enough to realize that this was about far more than an unusual bit of jewelry.

"You know," I said, "I don't mind losing a few battles, but I don't want to lose the war."

In retrospect it was a small matter, but for us it was a big step in our relationship. I was forced to begin to see my model-student-good-girl child as an adult with opinions I wouldn't always agree with, someone I couldn't always order around or persuade. She tried to placate me by saying she could always take it out and the skin would grow back, and while the ring eventually went away (which was never quite the door knocker I feared), she still has a small stud in her nose. And my dire predictions were unfounded. She earned her master's degree, has been a social worker and lived in Boston for about 27 years, and has been a positive contributor to her community. All with a nose ring that I could never quite understand and, as it turns out, don't need to.

Despite our continued persuasion, Paula and I have been unable to coax Ali to move back to Kansas City. Though as parents we all want to see our kids flourish and come into their own, it can still be a little bittersweet to relinquish a child to the world to live her own life, especially when that life is so far away. The distance may add challenges to keeping our relationship strong, but it continues to be one of the most important ones I'll ever have or want.

Our girls each had a few missteps as they matured, but not many, and in their careers they've both pursued professions where they've worked to improve a lot of people's lives. Mandi works as an early childhood educator for preschoolers with special needs, and Ali is a consultant with hospice care in the Boston area. With advanced degrees, they could have made a lot more money in different positions, but they have chosen professions and activities where they give back. They have even taken on extra work around the holidays so their Christian co-workers could spend Christmas with their families. They say they have been motivated by the examples of their parents, but being able to watch them lead their lives in such a way is a far greater honor.

If I'd known way back when what great adults they would grow up to be, I'd have had 10 more of them.

• • • •

We all have relationships with people on multiple levels: family, friends, employees, business partners, customers, advisors, professional networks. But our lives are so hectic that the time for developing relationships, particularly with those closest to us, often gets pushed to the side. It needs to be made a priority, highlighted by trust and open communication. A barrier to developing relationships is our expectation that everyone thinks like we do, but even among our closest relatives there are going to be different perceptions of the same things. The trick is to learn to accept and even celebrate those differences.

Make a point of scheduling time with those in your inner circle, whether business or personal, to learn more about them. Ask questions and be an effective listener who appreciates their positions and opinions. The rewards you receive in return will be many times greater than the time and effort that you've invested.

Chapter 9
GOALS: SEEING AND SCORING

Principle #9: Challenge yourself

*"Do not let what you cannot do
interfere with what you can do."*
John Wooden

When I was in Decatur in the 1980s, I became acquainted with a young man named Jim Phillips, who was a student at the University of Illinois. The youngest of 10 children in a Chicago family, he was a team manager and later became a student assistant for the Illini basketball team. He and I had gotten to know each other through my association with the team and had the opportunity to talk on several occasions about his ambitions, his career path, and the goals he was setting for his life. Right before he graduated, he sent me a letter of appreciation for the time we had spent together.

Jim wanted to be involved in coaching and soaked in everything he could from being around the Illinois coaching staff. He also was interested in a possible career in athletic administration and consulted with me to learn some principles of business. He epitomized what we would call a "goal-oriented" college student.

After Jim left Illinois he went to Arizona State, where he was a graduate assistant coach while he was working on his master's degree and then a full-time assistant before moving into administration in 1997. Later he went to Tennessee where he earned a Ph.D. in education administration and served as an assistant athletics director. From there he moved on to Notre Dame to become a senior associate athletics director for external affairs, before becoming director of athletics at Northern Illinois and then Northwestern. At every stop, he distinguished himself by his management and fundraising capabilities.

In February of 2021 Jim was named the Commissioner of the Atlantic Coast Conference, one of the most coveted college sports positions in the country. His résumé includes appointments to some of the most prestigious committees in college sports — including the Division I Men's Basketball Selection Committee, the NCAA Board of Governors, and the chairmanship of the inaugural NCAA Division I Council.

It's been quite a climb for the young man I first met in the late 1980s, and I've been proud as I've watched him develop, mature, and reach goal after goal. It's amazing what a person with purpose and focus can achieve.

• • • •

I always had a goal to stand out in a crowd. I learned early on when coming up through the ranks that I had to do whatever I could to distinguish myself, and I felt it gave me an edge. Maybe it meant volunteering for any task that a manager needed to have done or dressing in a professional manner that set me apart from the others. I did a reasonably good job selling cars, but I wasn't the top salesperson by a long shot. On the floor of the dealership selling cars was not the place I saw my future unfolding. Almost from the start, when I determined that the auto business would be my career, I set a goal for myself of getting into management and owning my own dealership.

But I knew that a goal by itself wasn't enough. It needed to be connected to action, to small, concrete goals that guided me to the larger one. In many ways, being part of the Van Tuyl organization set me up, not just to create a strong career, but to learn, almost by osmosis, how to avoid shortcuts, the value of putting people first, and, just as importantly, how to set a good goal for my own success. It had to be reachable but challenging, drawing me into the future and motivating. It had to inspire me to try unexpected paths and take risks.

I could see the structure was in place for me to do that in the Van Tuyl organization, and whenever they decided to make a change or a promotion, I wanted to be the one they thought of first. I'd get up every morning with the determination that I would be different from the others. I worked hard and trusted that I would get noticed.

My first management job was as the assistant to the assistant finance manager in 1974. All I did was take credit applications. I'd run around the dealership and work with the various salespeople, and when someone would buy a car I'd take the application for their loan as part of the package of paperwork. It wasn't much above a clerical position, and I was very low in the management ranks, but I wanted to be the person who did the best job at whatever they were asked to do.

Moving into management did entail some financial risk. At the time, I was selling enough cars to make $2,000 to $3,000 each month, which back then was decent money for someone just starting out. When I took the job in the finance department, I wasn't working directly with customers anymore and earning that commission, but the company did guarantee assistant managers about $1,200 per month to help stabilize things in the midst of the energy crisis. It was before we had children and Paula was teaching school, so we were at least in a position where I could take a pay cut and we would still be alright.

As it turned out, the guaranteed salary was a blessing. About this same time, the Arab Oil Embargo was taking root, which resulted in gas price hikes, long lines at the pumps, and lower speed limits on the highways. The U.S. automotive industry took a huge hit, especially as the Japanese were manufacturing more fuel-efficient cars. In light of all that, the guaranteed salary with a chance to keep climbing the corporate ladder didn't seem so bad. I was able to continue working on my goal of making it into management when many others would have had to shift or alter their goals and plans to achieve them.

It was a scary time in our industry, but I had two things going my way. First, I trusted our leadership when they reassured us that the organization would come out of this time in better shape. Secondly, I had a plan. Rather than being motivated by money, I was motivated by the opportunity for growth, which really made me the exception among people my age, certainly among my group of friends at the time. When I first moved back to Kansas City after college, a number of my fraternity brothers lived in the area, and we liked to go out on the town. It didn't take me long to understand that I couldn't make that a frequent part of my routine anymore, as I had been doing. I couldn't split my time and energy — I had to dedicate myself to my career and my family.

Even with that focus, if money had been my motivator, as a young man I probably would have chosen to stay in sales, even with the temporary slump in the industry. But that was not a strategy that could get me to where I wanted to go. Even then I saw myself as a person who could own a dealership, and I was confident that if I set my goals high enough the money would follow.

I had help along the way. While I was self-motivated enough to set parameters for my own life, I benefited from the experience and expertise of good managers who would sit down with me at the beginning of each month and help me set specific short-term goals for my department. I learned a lot in my early days that translated well for me when I became a general manager and eventually an owner. Depending on the position in a car dealership, goals can be set for gross profit, sales volume, or the number of calls a salesperson needs to make. In the service department, the goals are set for how long a technician takes to do an oil change, or at a higher level the time needed for a complicated job such as an engine overhaul. Every job is different, but still requires the setting of a goal.

In the days when things like GPS and cell phones were still the stuff of science fiction, I figured out quickly that using a road map was a necessity to reach a distant destination. When taking a long trip, we wouldn't just get up in the morning and say, "Here we go!" We'd have to know where we're going and use whatever tools were available to get there. Some time would be needed to develop a plan and an itinerary, both for the short- and long-term. Let's say we were traveling to Colorado. Our goal would be to get to our ultimate destination in 10 hours, but we'd also make plans to stop for gas and for lunch, or maybe just to take a break. We would look at the map and pay attention to signs along the way so we'd know we wouldn't be in the desolate wilds of western Kansas with no town in sight when we need refueling. Having career and life goals functions much the same way. We must look at likely pathways, choose a route, check for difficulties, and stay aware while we're on the road in case we need a course correction.

In practical terms, at our dealerships we have the managers turn in a plan each December on what they plan to do the following year to continue their success and move their individual departments forward. This includes an evaluation of their staffs, which may include additions to personnel. I also encourage them not to be regulated by mediocrity; if there's someone on their team who is just average, then they should consider ways to help them improve or finding a star to replace them.

From there I'll set a sales goal at the beginning of each month, and then use that to project a gross profit per car. We divide that up by the number of workdays in the month, and that's how many cars we have to sell in a day. Each salesperson is also given their own goal toward that end. When I was on the floor selling, I would set a goal of 15 or 20 cars each month, so if I went a few days without a sale, I knew I'd have to play catch up and maybe sell two cars in a day to hit that number.

In the automotive industry we use a daily operating control report for monitoring our goals on a short-term basis. The DOC is basically a 24-hour summary of information that drives the business. It obviously includes sales volumes and profit margins on cars, service, and parts, but it also measures worker productivity, monitors payroll and overhead, and assists in spotting trends. These trends help us set daily goals for each department and what they need to accomplish. However, those goals ebb and flow throughout the month and can be affected by conditions outside of our control and not represented on a data-driven document. If there's a snowstorm, for example, that may keep any department from reaching their daily goal, and, just as I did as a salesman, they may need play catch up to get back on track.

Because the path to achieving our long-term goals relies on the short-term objectives, we must be able to shift when something unexpected stands in our way. I like sports analogies, and the one that comes to mind here is the running back who has his head up. If the offensive lineman hasn't cleared a hole where it should be, the mediocre runner may just run into a big pile of people if he's not looking up. But the accomplished running back, whose eyes are wide open and taking in the whole picture, will spot where another hole has opened instead and pick up the needed yardage there. It's the same in life and in business. In paying attention to what's going on, you can adapt as you go. You have to be aware and seek the opportunities where they present themselves.

Cecil Van Tuyl preached "People, people, people," and keeping the needs of people, both customers and employees, foundational to the functioning of any business is necessary for success, but I would add two other key concepts: energy and net profit. As a department head, if you focus on those three components in your planning and goal setting, you'll have a successful team. Go out and find the best people, encourage them to bring energy to their jobs every day basis, and work to keep your department contributing to the net profit of the company.

And by net profit, I don't necessarily mean the dollars and cents, although we obviously need to make money to sustain the business. I'm talking about much more than that. Some departments, such as accounting and bookkeeping, are not going to directly improve the bottom line, as they require overhead without generating revenue. But their efforts and energy can still contribute to the overall success of the organization. To carry the football analogy a little further, those departments are like the offensive lineman whose name few people know, but he paves the way for the big-name running back or quarterback to make the plays that win the game. He may not be someone whom the public readily identifies, but the organization readily sees his value, and recognizes and compensates him for his contributions to a winning team.

An employee at any level needs to be able to see this value in themselves and in others. They alone have control of their areas and their tasks, and by exerting that control and making a goal for themselves they enhance the bottom line. A salesperson, a technician, an accountant, a receptionist — in any area someone can work hard and exceed the expectations of their job. A good manager sits down with their individual employees to develop a goal-oriented plan together for that individual's career.

When I got that job as an assistant to the assistant finance manager paying me $1,200 a month, I was committed to making the most of the opportunity, however slight it may have seemed. I had felt good about what I was doing when I was selling cars, but I knew I was an average salesperson, which meant being the best of the worst or the worst of the best. Either way, it wasn't a position from which I could achieve excellence or move forward. If I had been selling 30 cars a month, my superiors may have preferred that I stay in sales, and if I had been making a lot of money doing that, I might have chosen to pass on some of those non-sales opportunities as well. But once I had the opportunity to get into management and knew that I could find success there, I saw the upside of what the Van Tuyl organization could give me. I kept my eyes up and ran with the ball.

With my own new hires, I want to learn quickly whether

they just want to sell cars or if they have bigger goals in mind. I have several young guys in my organization who would like to be dealers, and the two who run my stores now — Jake Sacks and Randy Habiger — showed enough initiative and drive that I made them partners, and they have the first right of refusal to buy the dealerships if anything happens to me. They make a good living and own some stock in our company, which is a good investment for them. They're focused on their goals, and they are on track to benefit long-term. More than anything, I'm proud to be part of their career development, helping them set and achieve goals, just as Cecil did for me.

When I talk to someone who is just starting out in their career, I hope they look at me as I used to look at Cecil and my mentors. Back then, I understood that if I was smart, I'd figure out how to do what they asked of me, but I'd do it in my own way. Two different people looking at the same roadmap might still take two different paths to arrive at their destination successfully. If the instructions you're given by those above you are your road map, then you chart your path by the way you set and follow your goals. It's your determination to get up every morning, to come to work and do the best job you can even on the days when you don't have much energy, that will keep you on the road.

I like to share my story and pass on that experience. I want my employees to know these dealerships weren't given to me — that it took years of work to get where I am today, and I put that narrative into our employee manual. Those who pay attention and buy in not only succeed and grow in their position, but they also become salespeople for our brand, and everyone shares in the success.

• • • •

I try to have goals in every area of my life. I like to think I've succeeded in my desire to be a good husband, father, and grandfather. I've had 50 years' worth of a strong marriage, characterized by honesty and support. I have great relationships with my two wonderful and productive daughters who are independent, capable, and loving. And I have a grandson who's my best buddy. The achievement of family goals also relies on the goals and actions of other people, and I know I've been luckier than most in that regard.

And then there is our family's venture into the wine business, which started as a passion project and has entailed a whole new set of goals. Originally, I wanted a nice bottle of wine in my name or the company's name as a gift I could give to customers and friends for their enjoyment. I partnered with a winery in St. Paul, Oregon, named Lady Hill Winery. The more I got to know the business the more goals I set and the more committed I became, and I eventually became the principal owner. We now have the Miles Bordeaux, the Beebe Chardonnay, the Sisters Blanc de Noirs, the Schnaer Family Wines Pinot Noir, and two Chalmers blends (created in partnership with the family of former Kansas and NBA guard Mario Chalmers), all under the umbrella of Schnaer Family Wines.

When entering the wine business, one should understand up front that it probably won't make money. (There's a lot of truth in the old joke that if you want to make a million dollars in the wine business you should start with two.) A lot of your success is determined by the distributors, the state and federal liquor laws, and of course the consumer, who has thousands of different choices. To have a quality product you also can produce only a limited number of cases each year, and you're always at the mercy of the weather.

My business goals had to be different than they were for the dealerships. I needed a different roadmap. Along this path I have developed a passion for wine and set a goal to learn as much as I can about the industry, with two objectives: producing a quality product and eventually becoming a sommelier myself. But as much as I'm invested in this enterprise, I determined from the beginning that I wouldn't compromise my dealerships by taking money out of my main business to prop up the winery. The winery must remain a venture that can stand on its own. And so far, so good.

• • • •

Whatever one's dreams or expectations may be, setting goals helps us plan our journey. Some goals can be accomplished in a day, and no matter how small or insignificant they may seem, there is still a feeling of pride in reaching them. Other goals may require an entire lifetime, and we still may not reach them, but the striving can itself be valuable, pushing us to new heights.

It's never too early in life to start setting goals. We can begin by asking ourselves, "What do I want for my life?" Above all, in setting these goals we must consider what will make us happy in the long term. This means that our ultimate reward should not be accumulation of money or material goods, but rather what ultimately gives us the most satisfaction. The goal may be "Someday I want to own my own business" or "I want to be healthy and fit." Or it could be as simple as "I want to help others and make those around me happy." Wealth can help achieve these goals, but it should be a tool or a byproduct. As a motivating factor, it will eventually fall short and leave you unfulfilled.

Once the long-term goal is identified, then it's time to break it down and think about what we want to accomplish in the short term (e.g., today, tomorrow, next month, next year). In my case, I set the goal of having my own dealership, and then in the short term to move from the sales floor into management, even if it resulted in a cut in pay. As part of my long-term plan, a short-term goal was to learn from my supervisors how to effectively run a dealership. I also advise looking at an intermediate plan — maybe something spanning five years or so — and adjusting it periodically as both professional and personal circumstances change.

For example, when faced with the COVID-19 pandemic beginning in 2020, the whole world was faced with an uncontrollable outside factor that, one way or another, was going to affect our lives and our businesses. At Crown Automotive, we were uncertain about the immediate future and what it would do to our in-person traffic, and there was a temporary lull in sales that caused us to reassess our goals for the year. But we did not alter our core philosophy or long-term dealership goals. After the initial public health response, we found that people wanted to get back out and travel. They weren't going to get on an airplane or a bus, so they looked at buying a car to travel to the Ozarks or the Flint Hills of Kansas or a camp in a national park. After that initial slump, sales rebounded and were solid.

However, the semiconductor supply shortage impacted dealerships much more as it became difficult to get inventory. I'm sure initially it looked like our business was waning since we had so few cars on the lot, but once customers understood it was an industry-wide problem, they learned that they could still get what they wanted — they may just have to wait a few weeks or months to get something specific. But the cars we did get in sold immediately, and even the semiconductor shortage days have been stable. They weren't like we planned, but we adjusted our short-term goals and projections and made it work.

Writing goals down is also an effective tool, as long as the pages are not thrown in a file and put out of sight. In business, we keep our goals at the forefront of meetings and on our agendas. In our personal lives, having clearly stated, black and white goals is no less effective. Referring back to the written word can be a consistent reminder of where we are relative to where we want to go. It can give us a deadline and keep us accountable.

Finally, in setting goals it is important that they be challenging yet attainable. It is self-defeating to make them unrealistic but setting them too easy provides little motivation or incentive to reach for anything bold or ambitious. Deadlines should be set, the details should be specific, and, in business, the communication of them must be clear to every member of the organization.

Goals give us a road map to life and success. You can't just wake up and hope. Hope is not a plan.

MAX

If you're not familiar with the name of Max Falkenstien, then you haven't spent much time around the Midwest or college sports. For 60 years he was the radio color commentator for the University of Kansas men's basketball and football teams. To put that number in perspective, he's only surpassed by Vin Scully, the legendary voice of the Brooklyn and Los Angeles Dodgers, for longevity as an announcer with one team. That is rare company indeed.

When I first took over the dealerships in Lawrence, Bob Billings, a real estate developer, and Bill "Dolph" Simons, owner of the local paper and cable tv company, both got me involved in the Lawrence Chamber of Commerce. There I was able to meet a lot of the movers and shakers in the area.

At one of the Chamber luncheons, I was heading to the end of the buffet line and passed Max, who was already near the front of the line. He grabbed me as I walked by. Through another area car dealer, I had already been introduced to the KU athletic department's courtesy car program, which was similar to the one I had participated in for the University of Illinois. Max, as the longtime voice of the Jayhawks, apparently had heard about me through that connection.

"You're the new dealer in town. Get right up here in front of me," he said, and with some degree of embarrassment I cut into line in front of a number of other people.

We chatted a lot that day and that started a decades-long friendship. We weren't particularly close at the start, but our friendship grew, and we would go to lunch about once a week to talk sports in general and Kansas basketball in particular. Max always went for the hamburger and fries, and he couldn't understand why I ate salads, which is my usual fare. The one time I did indulge myself in a burger and fries it felt practically sinful, and Max gave me lots of grief.

Max's father, Earl, had been the business manager for the KU athletic department for 33 years, so Max had deep roots with the university and the community. He had started in radio and worked for local stations for a number of years, eventually joining Douglas County Bank as a senior vice president and spokesman, while continuing to broadcast games on the side. He did some "Games of the Week" for the old Big Eight Conference back in the 1960s, but really made his name on Jayhawk football and basketball broadcasts. Starting in 1946 and continuing until his retirement in 2006, he covered more than 1,750 basketball games and 650 football games. A jersey with his name and the number 60, recognizing the number of years he spent on the broadcasts, hang among the retired Kansas numbers in Allen Fieldhouse. He is the only non-player to have his "jersey" honored in the rafters.

Max retired from his bank job at the end of 1994, and not long after that my switchboard called one day to let me know he was in the dealership and wanted to see me. He asked for a few minutes of my time, so I brought him into my office.

"I have a proposal," he said. "I need a car. It doesn't have to be fancy and doesn't have to be new. But if you can help me out,

Mom and Dad set me on the right path at an early age. I couldn't have asked for more loving parents.

Clothes clearly do make the man. This suit wasn't custom-made, but I've always tried to be a sharp dresser.

My father worked long hours and would even fill prescriptions through his lunch hours at the pharmacy. His exemplary work ethic continues to inspire me today.

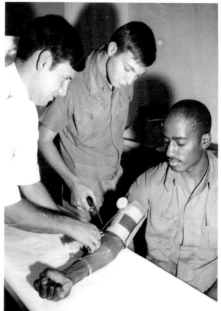

In the Army, I was part of the medical group known as the "blood suckers." This piqued my interest in medical school, but that dream wasn't to be.

It was a close call, but I did manage to graduate from Pittsburg State, which pleased my parents, Paula, and even a professor or two.

In the early '70s, I took my stylish wide ties to the finance department of Van Chevrolet. This gave me an opportunity to learn a different side of the business.

Illinois Assistant Coach Dick Nagy was a loyal friend of mine through thick and thin. My daughters and Paula also enjoyed having him visit our home in Decatur.

Children in need have always been a motivator for me. In Decatur, we worked with the local hospital foundation to supply sleep monitors to underprivileged kids with medical issues.

Nick Anderson of the Fighting Illini went on to a long NBA career. He and other players were customers of mine in Decatur (with all transactions handled aboveboard).

It's always great to celebrate with the staff at the grand opening of a new dealership, especially with my beautiful wife there to cut the ribbon.

Paula and I had a lot to celebrate when I was named the 2001 Time Dealer of the Year for the state of Kansas.

When I lost my good friend and business partner, Dale Backs, I commissioned Van Go, Inc. to create this bench in his memory.

Sitting front and center with the 2008 NCAA Champion Kansas Jayhawks was a thrill and an honor.

My eyes were fixed on the road during the Jayhawks' championship parade as I carried precious cargo — the Most Outstanding Player of the 2008 Final Four, Mario Chalmers.

These rings — one for Illinois' 1984 Big Ten Championship and the other for Kansas' 2008 NCAA title — are among my most cherished items of memorabilia.

One of the best years of our lives was when Maddox and Mandi lived with us when he was about 2 years old. He was and remains a good buddy.

I married into a great family. Paula's parents, James and Jean Beebe, have been wonderful grandparents to Ali and Mandi. Unfortunately, James passed away in 2021.

I was an annoying brother, but my big sisters always looked out for me. Sadly, we lost Bonnie (left) to pancreatic cancer in 2018, and Madeline has struggled with health issues in recent years.

Max Falkenstien spent 60 years behind the microphone for KU athletics — and became a close friend to me in his later years.

I've maintained my fitness so that I can still complete some races, including this one that turned from a 5K into a 10K when I made a wrong turn.

In 2017, I joined a group of KU supporters for Bill Self's induction into the Naismith Hall of Fame in Springfield, Massachusetts. Front Row: Scott Ward (KU Associate AD for Student-Athlete Development), Sherron Collins (member of KU's 2008 NCAA championship team), Doug Compton Jr., Mike Christie. Back Row: Robert Green, David Ball, me.

It was an honor to be named a laureate in the 2017 class inducted into the Lawrence Business Hall of Fame. My speech followed a flattering introduction by 11-year old Mavrick Hawkins (center).

I'm surrounded by outstanding teammates at the Crown dealerships. Smiles are all around as we celebrate another great year at our annual holiday party.

I prefer salads to hot dogs, but I couldn't turn down my good friend Rabbi Zalman Tiechtel when I visited KU's Chabad Jewish Center concession stand at Allen Fieldhouse with my attorney, John Hampton.

My love of wines led to the beginning of Schnaer Family Wines. Our *Sisters Blanc de Noirs* is one of our signature blends, in tribute to Ali (left) and Mandi.

I continue to enjoy spending time with friends from my formative years in Kansas City, especially my lifelong buddy, Larry Spitcaufsky, and his sister, Nancy Eisner.

Making friends like Cole Browne has been an extra benefit I've enjoyed from my association with Cottonwood, Inc., which supports adults with developmental disabilities.

Recognition for our dealerships, in this case with the katana sword awarded by Toyota, becomes a habit when you have general managers like Randy Habiger (left) and Jake Sacks.

I can't talk or think about family for too long without my eyes getting misty. Ali, Mandi (with her dog, Bella), Maddox, and Paula make life pretty special.

Golf has provided a lot of enjoyment and made me many friends over the years, plus it has given me the opportunity to play at famous courses, such as here at Pebble Beach.

Paula set me on the path to success and has been my best friend and companion for more than 50 years.

I'd be happy to be a spokesman for the dealership and do your commercials."

I felt like I had won the lottery. I couldn't believe that in all his years no other car dealer had hired him to do their ads or promotional work. In eastern Kansas, being with Max was like being with Elvis or Cher or Bono — everyone knew him and referred to him only by his first name. I could have given him any car on the lot and it would have been well worth it in exchange for what he did for me. After that our friendship really grew. I even convinced him do the greeting for the voicemail on my cell phone.

When Kansas won the 2008 NCAA Tournament in San Antonio, Max had already retired from the broadcast booth and was no longer traveling with the team. I decided to splurge and chartered a plane to take four of us there, including Max, but when we got to the airfield our mode of transportation wasn't quite what I had envisioned. It was such a tiny plane that I had to sit in the copilot's seat and Max was stuck in the back with luggage on his lap.

During that Final Four weekend, while we were walking around the Riverwalk in San Antonio, I felt like I was in Max's entourage. Everywhere we went people came up to talk to him. He was a true legend.

When it was time to come back from San Antonio, we saw Dick Vitale, the former coach and fabled ESPN analyst at the airport. He and Max had known each other for years, and of course they struck up a conversation. Dick was about to board a fancy Gulfstream Private Jet — probably furnished by the network, and I think Max was a little self-conscious about climbing into our little puddle jumper. He pulled me aside and asked if we could delay our departure until Dick's plane had already taken off. I chuckled, but understood, and promised the next time I would make sure we had a more comfortable plane.

Max passed away in 2019 at the age of 95. He was one of the greatest people I've ever known. In his last years he had to go to dialysis three times a week, and along with some other friends I chipped in to drive when his family needed assistance. Even as his health began to fail, we maintained our regular lunch meetings, where he continued to eat the fried and greasy meals while I enjoyed my salads. "That's criminal," he'd say about my diet, and he'd occasionally still remind me about that one time I had a burger.

Even though he's gone I still have him as the voice on my cell phone. After his passing, I asked his son Kurt if it would be okay for me to do that, and he said Max would have been honored. It catches people by surprise when they first hear it, but I know it brings a smile to their faces. Sometimes I just play it for myself so I can hear his voice.

"This is Max. I don't know where Miles is, but if I can find him, I'll have him call you."

Rest in peace, Max. Your voice is still strong in my life and in the lives of those you touched along your journey.

Chapter 10
"DO SOMETHING"

Principle #10: Be involved and
be active in the community

"Don't just stand there taking up space."
The Eagles

I've always liked the Eagles, and the lyrics of their song "Do Something" really resonate with me. Recorded in 2007 as a track on their last studio album, Long Road Out of Eden, the song starts with a reference to a failed relationship that has the singer feeling like giving up, but a voice inside him asks, "Why don't you do something?"

The song moves beyond this one relationship, however. In an interview with Billboard magazine the year the album debuted, co-writer Don Henley said the following:

> 'Do Something' is an interesting song because it starts out like a love song…but then it takes on larger implications. And that line ("How did we get on this road we are traveling?") could pertain

to a relationship between a man and a woman
or it could be a statement about the country as
a whole.

There are a lot of ideas packed into those lyrics, but ultimately the point is very straightforward. Basically, you must decide to take action, and it's never too late to start.

For me it pertains to a daily approach to my life. I just can't sit around and be a bump on a log, hoping that something good is going to happen. I was raised and mentored by hard workers who also cared deeply about those around them and seemed tireless in their activities, and it's a method of living that has certainly taken root in my own life, both as a business philosophy and as a principle of philanthropy. If I'm going to do something, I need to go full speed ahead — a halfhearted effort will never be enough to make a real difference. In both our personal and business lives, we don't simply find ourselves in the right place; we put ourselves in the right place. I have to "do something."

As strong as my early influences were, I wasn't always that type of person. As a kid I wanted to play sports and be the best, and I always tried to be a leader on my teams, but otherwise, I was complacent growing up. I took saxophone and clarinet lessons, and I sang in the youth choir, but I eventually dropped those activities because I preferred being outside with my buddies. I have some regrets about that now. I tried to learn to piano as an adult in order to play for my mom's 100th birthday, but I wish I'd let Mom and Dad convince me to try harder with some of those activities when I was young. Our parents are smarter than we can ever give them credit for when we're kids.

I also wasn't a good student and didn't really try to be. I don't have to try to give my grandson much encouragement in his studies, because my daughter is an educator, and she makes sure that her son hits the books. As he gets older, though, I will encourage him to stay true to the path he decides on for his life, to find what he wants to do and be happy with it, whatever it is. Sometimes I think that if I had applied myself more in school, I probably wouldn't be in the car business now. I might even have achieved that medical career my mother had hoped for. But once I made that commitment to do something, I began to feel comfortable, and success followed.

For all my lack of effort in my youth, I know I'm pretty lucky and blessed to be where I am today, because my practice of "doing something" didn't really begin to take root until I made the commitment in my relationship with Paula and to my career. I'm thankful in retrospect that she put the reality of our relationship so bluntly. At the time it felt a bit like an ultimatum; if she hadn't put it that way, I fear I would have just meandered along with a limited sense of direction.

Working in the Van Tuyl organization also taught me not to be content with drifting along and just maintaining what I was doing. It didn't take me long to realize that I needed to do more or I wouldn't be successful and, as a result, I'd be looking for another place to work. In that company nobody would succeed by just showing up and hoping for the best.

• • • •

While that set me on the right path for a career and got me in the mode of "doing something" professionally, until I lived in Decatur I was not particularly involved in community or charitable events. At that point I just wanted to sell cars. I was working not just for myself but for Cecil. He was involved in a few causes, but he wasn't public about it. And at this stage of my career, I pretty much emulated him. He went to work to work, and I took that to heart.

It was at the behest of the guy who did the advertising and promotion for my Decatur dealerships, a fellow by the name of Bob Nichols of R.A. Nichols Advertising, that this began to shift. Around 1983 he came to me and said, "It's time for you to get involved."

Now, we had sponsored baseball teams and provided hole-in-one cars for charitable golf tournaments, and I tried to spread my monetary donations around as much as I could without going bankrupt, but Bob wanted me to do more in the community. He explained that there were organizations that could use my expertise and perspective, not just my money, and as a responsible member of the community it was incumbent on me to contribute my "time, talent, and treasure." As an added bonus, it would also likely benefit my businesses.

Much like Paula's "ultimatum," Bob's urge to act really struck a chord with me. At this time the economy had rebounded from the malaise of the late 1970s, so my dealerships were really starting to do well, and I felt like I had a little room to breathe. "Let me stick my toe in the water," I told him, "and I'll see how it goes."

The first organization with which I became involved was Milliken University, and later I supported the Decatur Chamber of Commerce, the local YMCA, and the area chapters of the American Cancer Society and the Muscular Dystrophy Association. This first experience of stretching beyond my own concerns, business or otherwise, was a turning point in how I saw myself and my purpose and how I used my time and efforts. I began to feel, more than just know, that I could make a difference. I saw the faces and knew the names of people who could be helped, lives that could be made better, by just a little effort on my part. It was simultaneously powerful and humbling to think I could have that kind of positive influence on my community. Getting active in these causes and seeing the effects really whetted my appetite for more. As a result, I dove in further and helped set up foundations at two area hospitals.

A significant opportunity surfaced soon afterward with the Gus Macker 3-on-3 Basketball Tournament, an inclusive event that benefits local charities wherever it's held. Started in 1974 in Lowell, Michigan, where the streets were closed off and turned into basketball courts, it has since spread to about 75 cities nationwide. At the time, I was the president of our Chevrolet Ad Association for Central Illinois. Our lead Chevrolet advertising agency was out of Michigan and had been involved with the Macker Tournament there, and they approached us about sponsoring a Macker Tournament in our area.

The group sponsorship didn't work out, but given my lifelong love of the game, I felt a particular connection to the association and was determined to bring the tournament to Decatur, so I approached the lead agency and told them I would be willing to be the sole sponsor. We closed the streets downtown over a Labor Day weekend and attracted more than a thousand teams. To keep the associated money circulating in the town, I designated as beneficiaries the two hospitals where I had set up foundations. It remained a popular annual event that ran for 15 years in Decatur, until I moved back to Kansas City.

Once I had set up shop with my dealerships in Lawrence, I thought the Macker Tournament would be a natural fit there as well. After all, we have a rich basketball tradition dating back to James Naismith, the game's founder and the first coach at the University of Kansas, and the success of

Jayhawk basketball is known throughout the country. Before I could bring the tournament to Lawrence, however, I learned that Cottonwood, Inc. had established a committee to start a 3-on-3 basketball tournament in Lawrence. I knew several members of the committee, including a couple of bankers and Roger Morningstar, a former Kansas player, and I told the organization's CEO that I had experience with this type of event and wanted to be involved.

Without hesitation she said, "Why don't you just be the major sponsor?" However, this would require a $7,000 donation. I hesitated at first because in Decatur we were able to cover costs with donations from multiple businesses, and we were still new in Lawrence and didn't yet have the same community connections. I decided to commit, though, and the dealerships were the major sponsor, not only for that year but for all three years the tournament was held.

Over that time, I became acquainted with the staff and clientele at Cottonwood and was increasingly impressed with their mission and operation. Their management knew that I had an affinity for their type of organization, and they asked me to join the board of directors, and I happily agreed. The next year they were looking for a chairperson for a fundraiser displaying a designer showcase house. Paula had chaired a similar project in Decatur, and she agreed to handle that one. She did a great job, and the success of that venture put us on the map in the Lawrence business and philanthropic circles. That event spawned a three-day wine festival, for which Paula and I were co-chairs, followed in that position by former Kansas City Chief Kendall Gammon and his wife. We stayed involved with that charity function for 18 years before stepping aside in 2020.

Cottonwood provides gainful employment to their clients and has secured contracts with businesses and the U.S. government to assemble and package various products. One of the most successful projects is the production of cargo tie-down straps for the Department of Defense, for which Cottonwood has now supplied more than 8 million units. Cottonwood also sets up group homes where their clients can live safely and with independence, so they are not institutionalized.

I love the time I'm able to spend with Cottonwood patrons and clients who are supported each day in maintaining their job skills and interacting with the community. They are an engaging group of people, and the friendships and associations I have made there have provided a tenfold return on any contributions I've been able to make. It seems serendipitous now that I became involved with them, and I can trace the roots of it back to Decatur and Gus Macker. I would have missed out of so much if I'd been happy to simply stick to my job and leave the community work and philanthropy to someone else with more time or more money or more inherent connection or whatever excuses we tend to give.

In addition to my support of agencies that serve those with disabilities, I've also found tremendous gratification in aiding organizations that promote youth activities. One opportunity to improve access to youth sports in Lawrence came about through my affiliation with the University of Kansas basketball program, again seemingly serendipitously.

I quickly developed a friendship with Bill Self after he succeeded Roy Williams as KU's men's basketball coach in 2003. After the Jayhawks won the 2008 NCAA Championship, he appreciated my involvement so much that he invited me to sit next to him in a team picture, and I also received a championship ring in recognition of my support for the team.

A short time after that championship season, my receptionist said that Bill Self was on the line to talk to me. I thought somebody was probably pulling my leg, but when I picked up the phone, I immediately recognized his voice. He asked if I had some time to meet with him.

Bill, it turned out, had an idea for a venture he hoped I would care about as much as he did. Bill's son, Tyler, who played on the team at Kansas from 2012 to 2017, was in junior high when the Jayhawks won the national championship in '08, and he had participated in youth basketball in the area. Surprisingly, in spite of our basketball roots, the facilities for youth sports were sorely lacking, particularly in a town of almost 100,000 citizens with a major university. The fact that Tyler, and for that matter any young athlete from the Lawrence area, had to be transported 30 miles away to play in Topeka was not acceptable to Bill, and I couldn't help but see his point.

Bill and his wife, Cindy, had started the Assists Foundation to help organizations in fundraising for a variety of youth activities. Their mission was to promote healthy lifestyle programs facilitated by education, assessments, leadership, prevention, and competition. It was now time for their big initiative.

Bill asked for 15 minutes of my time, but our meeting lasted about two hours as we enthusiastically dove into the discussion. He outlined his desire to help jumpstart a youth recreational center in Lawrence, and he wanted my help. Working with the city and other donors, the Foundation originally pledged $1 million toward the total cost of $24.5 million, but through our efforts and matching donations, we were able to increase that to $2 million. The facility, which opened in 2014, features basketball and volleyball courts, weight and cardio rooms, indoor soccer fields, outdoor tennis courts, and walking/jogging tracks both indoor and out. I was more than happy to lend my efforts and expertise to the venture, setting up fundraisers and meeting with potential donors to find matching funds to support the Foundation.

But our efforts went far beyond just the construction of facilities. We gave scholarships and grants to organizations that were helping underprivileged youth find opportunities through sports and education. We provided four $10,000 awards every year to kids in the Lawrence and Kansas City, Kansas school districts to attend college. The recipients were motivated students of high achievement but had little if any financial means to continue their education. When Bill and Cindy weren't available, I would go to the schools to present the scholarship awards, and I was privileged to meet some great young people from tough backgrounds who were being given a chance to really make something of themselves.

These young people had to struggle to experience the things that I'd taken almost for granted as a cared-for, middle-class kid. I'd been unmotivated but had opportunities all around me. They had few of those opportunities but all the drive in the world, and I could see how much it meant to them to be given this chance. I don't think they could see how much it meant to me to be part of their journey.

Another youth-centric local organization that I've supported in Lawrence is Van Go, which sponsors a nationally recognized employment program rooted in the arts. The organization serves teens and young adults, ages 14-24, who may come from a difficult home environment or have had some emotional struggles in their lives. Many of their participants offer testimonials about how Van Go kept them from dropping out of high school, or even from harming themselves, and provided them the motivation to attend college or pursue a career in the arts. A major initiative of theirs in the community is the creation of colorfully unique benches, a few of which I've purchased for our dealerships, including the one in memory of Dale Backs.

I've been interviewed by Van Go's marketing arm several times for their promotional materials as to why I'm involved and why I provide financial support and help with products and services for their art projects. It's an easy question to answer. Once you hear one of these kid's testimonials it just grabs you. Their motivation to improve their lives in turn motivates me. They do more for me than I can ever do for them.

The more often I can lend a helping hand to an individual who may have had some curves thrown at them early in their life, the more certain I am that that's a big part of why God put me on this earth and has given me gifts to share. I know I was put here for a purpose, and a life consumed by self-indulgence is not the path to happiness, neither for me nor anyone I might influence. Bringing joy to others is.

There have been other causes along the way that have also been close to my heart. I'm still on the Foundation Board at Pittsburg State, and when I first moved back to Kansas City to take over the Auto Plaza, I started the Brad Schifman Foundation as a memorial to my nephew who died of leukemia at the age of 28, in order to encourage and perpetuate the bone marrow registry. There was also the Kansas City Sports Walk of Fame and a stint on the board of the Special Olympics. My past experiences, my family, and my passions continue to inform the causes that take root with me, but above all it's the people. I give money, time, and expertise, but what I receive back cannot be measured on the same scales.

• • • •

Professionally speaking, active participation in trade organizations has been important to me as well. I've served on the General Motors Presidents Council and the Toyota National Dealers' Advisory Council, which work on a worldwide basis to promote those specific companies and dealerships. The Kansas Automobile Dealers Association and the Illinois Automobile Dealers Association, both of whose boards I have been a member of, raise money for political candidates and try to make sure the concerns of our section of the industry are heard and understood when legislation is being made.

For example, during the days of the General Motors bankruptcy in the late 2000s, there were members of Congress who were saying that the individual dealerships were costing the manufacturers money and that, in effect, we should restructure or eliminate car dealers. But dealers own everything about their businesses except the rights to the franchise, so it doesn't cost the manufacturers to work with us; in fact, it makes them money because the dealers buy the cars. So we had to talk to the administration, under President Obama at the time, and help them understand that it wasn't the dealership structure causing the layoffs and bankruptcies. We were successful, and they rethought proposed legislation that would have ended up being harmful to the entire industry and especially to the dealers.

It may not be as obviously charitable as some of my other activities, but I can still see these efforts making a difference in people's lives. Without these organizations' intervention, the industry would have been damaged, people would have lost livelihoods, and families would have suffered. My voice alone would have carried little weight, but as an active member and leader in the state dealerships' associations I was able to leverage the collective strength of many dealers to help educate legislators and stop the enactment of what would have been onerous regulations.

• • • •

Paula says I can't say no to anybody, and her voice rings in my ear every time I get a new request for involvement. For the most part, she's right, but I have had to learn to be somewhat selective, because when I do get involved in any entity, I'm all in. I've been asked to be on boards for hospitals, libraries, and similar types of not-for-profit organizations, and I've had to respectfully decline, even though I admire their missions and aims.

Through the dealerships we do fund a lot of sponsorships that don't require active participation, among them the local Boys and Girls Club, the Junior Achievement of Lawrence, and both the Chabad Center for Jewish Life and KU Hillel on the University of Kansas campus. Now we're also helping Pittsburg State by making contributions to perpetuate the mission of the university, which for obvious reasons is a special place for our family. But I've only been able to do that as I've accumulated some personal wealth over the last few years.

As far as personal participation, however, I don't want to just sit on a committee or board, and I'm not there just to get my name on the letterhead or website. I want to be active and out front, and a lot of times that means taking on a leadership role. Many businesspeople don't commit to participation in outside organizations and use the excuse that it takes valuable time away from the management of their companies. It's a valid point, and one for which I am not going to criticize anyone. But the rewards of activity are plentiful. There have even been numerous studies showing that volunteering time and/or donating money improves health and happiness. Assisting others can increase life expectancy and lower blood pressure, provide a sense of purpose, and influence the involvement of others. The bottom line for me is that it makes me feel good.

In addition to the fact that helping others helps satisfy a need in me, there are several professional and interpersonal benefits to being actively involved in the community and supporting charitable organizations, just as Bob Nichols told me all those years ago in Decatur. They have long since stopped being a primary motivation for involvement, but it would be dishonest to say it's not still a nice bonus and part of a sound business model. I continue to find that community and philanthropic engagement expands my circle of influence and provides opportunities to make friends and contacts outside of my regular group of associates. I love meeting new people, and that can't help but be good for my business. Almost everyone needs to buy a car someday, and when they do I want them thinking about Crown dealerships. I also might develop a new connection with an individual who has experienced a business or personal challenge similar to one I may be confronting, and I might learn something that will aid in my decision making.

Relationships with institutions such as a Chamber of Commerce help keep me apprised of developments in the area that can directly impact my stores. I would prefer to be on the front end of information disbursement when a new employer is coming to the area, or if there is a highway or road project that might impede traffic to and from my dealership locations. If I wait until I read it in the paper, then it might already be too late to influence it or adjust to meet it.

Participation in state and national industry associations also puts me in a position to have my opinions heard on regulations that can affect my industry. These types of organizations also provide resources for education and professional development and serve as clearinghouses to sift through trade publications for the most relevant information for improving our business. Over the years I've been especially active in these associations, and it does require a significant time commitment, but I like to think it's been a mutually beneficial relationship. I've been honored to be recognized as the *Time* magazine Dealer of the Year in both Illinois and Kansas. Twice during my tenure, I was one of eight dealers in the country who were selected to go to Japan, where we would meet with Toyota engineers, learn the culture of the company, and huddle with their executives. They were fascinating chances for learning and valuable opportunities to expand our global perspective.

• • • •

I advise people to pursue activities in the areas they're most passionate about — in my case that turned out to be with youth and people with disabilities. If you're hesitant to get involved, or just unsure of how to go about it, I can offer a few practical suggestions. First, if you're new to a community, look at websites operated by the town or city that list upcoming events. Almost every town has a chamber of commerce, which is an easy way for a business to build its associations with other companies and not-for-profit organizations. Second, talk to new friends and neighbors about organizations they support and about how you might get involved. Also look for volunteer opportunities associated with a church or synagogue. Almost without exception, religious institutions will have affiliations with charitable groups. And communities of any size will have donation centers, thrift stores, soup kitchens, homeless housings, or animal shelters. Many of these organizations and associations will post frequent updates on social media (like Facebook, Twitter, and Nextdoor), so don't forget to check groups' sites for volunteer openings. As I learned, one opportunity tends to lead to another as your passions and expertise drive you forward into a position to make a difference that is unique to you, a difference that only you can make.

And while it's important to provide financial assistance, there needs to be more to our charitable engagements. From an effort standpoint, writing a check is easy, especially when we have plenty of resources. But your greatest gift is often your time and your talent, and that requires genuine engagement. A person can write checks, but if they're not truly involved they really can't make a difference and the experience can't make a difference for them. You have to get up and go "do something."

A few years ago, when I was on the Lawrence Chamber of Commerce Board of Directors, I had to miss some meetings because we had been traveling. When I returned, I told Cathy Lewis, who at the time was on the Chamber staff, that I was sorry I had been unable to attend for a while.

"We definitely missed you," she said. "You just don't know the effect you have on the people in this boardroom when you're here."

I told her it was very nice of her to say — I certainly want people to know I care, and if there's something I can do to help them financially or with my time, I'm glad they know I'm willing to do it.

Her comment caught me by surprise and stuck with me, though, and I've thought about it a lot in the ensuing years. We're all busy people and it's easy to get consumed by our own activities, even when they're charitable, and get bogged down in the minutiae, the to do lists, the practicalities. The passion can start to wane, and people burn out without the motivation of past days. We seldom get to see ourselves and our efforts through other people's eyes. Being able to do so, in that small way and in that small moment, helped remind me that there's grace present every time we "do something," even when that something is just a committee meeting. Even our simplest and most mundane of efforts, when offered with a giving spirit and enthusiasm, are important to those around us. No work is wasted.

Chapter 11
THE ITCH

Principle #11: Have intensity,
tenacity, curiosity, and humility

"Happiness is having a scratch for every itch."
Ogden Nash

It's probably obvious by now that it's hard for me to sit
still — that I stay active in numerous ways and am always
looking for something to keep me challenged. I have an itch to
keep life moving along. I think it boils down to a combination
of four traits I commonly see in successful people and try to
foster in myself: intensity, tenacity, curiosity, and humility.
The more of each of these traits I can develop in myself — the
greater my ITCH grows — the more impact and success I can
have in my career and my community.

INTENSITY

A single candle generates one small flame, but that flame can
be used to light a thousand other candles without shortening

the life of the original. In turn, each of those candles can light a thousand more.

Intensity can be equally contagious. However much one intense person may be able to accomplish, when their attitude radiates among a group of people with a common goal and the underlying motivation to succeed, the capacity for action and change will increase exponentially. And it's a self-feeding flame. The more success that they have, the more confident they become. That confidence can then fuel a greater desire for success and a corresponding increase in their intensity, and the cycle begins again.

I sometimes equate it with a sports team on a winning streak. With each win players become more confident, and that confidence translates into energy. That energy keeps that team laser-focused on preparation for the next game, so they're even more ready for the next opponent they meet.

In Decatur, I was in a running group with several friends. It started off as more of a social gathering as we came together for some short runs, but our collective intensity motivated us to increase our distance until we were knocking out five and 10 miles at a time. We started running some 5K and 10K races, and from there our competitive instincts pushed us even farther. Several of us set a goal to run a marathon, and I was all in. I ran every day and was gradually increasing my mileage until I was ready for a marathon in the fall. An injury prevented me from participating in the actual race when the time came, but I never regretted the time and energy I spent on the preparation. I will never know what my final time might have been, but being part of that group, spurring one another on to greater achievement, was an experience I'm glad I had.

Within a group, intensity can motivate teams and individuals to reach goals far above what they ever thought they could do on their own. Regarding outside competition, intensity keeps organizations and teams from becoming complacent. The intensity among competitors in any field will vary with a number of factors, and it's key that the participants are aware of them. How many competitors are there to keep track of? Are there barriers to becoming a true competitor, such as high fixed costs or technical expertise, that may need to be tackled first? Is the product involved viewed as a commodity with little differentiation among suppliers, making the consumer particularly price-sensitive? Answers to such questions will help teams — or organizations — decide where to focus their intensity to make the most efficient use of it.

Two types of competition with which I am particularly familiar are sports and, naturally, the automobile business. Of course, competition in athletics is particularly intense — in most sports there is only one champion when the season comes to an end. A team or an individual can have a great season, but if they lose in the playoffs or championship game, someone else will take the ultimate prize. In college and professional leagues, millions of dollars are spent to attract the best executives, coaches, and players. They're in the "get it right" business, and when those in charge don't get it right (i.e., consistently contend for a championship) changes are often made. The rewards can be great — schools and franchises make millions of dollars, prestige is earned, players find opportunities for greater recognition and, eventually, paychecks — but the negative consequences can be arduous and are usually played out in a public forum. It's an industry that requires incredibly intense competitors because there's so much so visibly at stake.

The competition is not quite that intense among auto dealerships, as more than one can be a winner. We all can have good years without anyone going home a loser, and there is also a great deal of collaboration in the functioning of our professional trade associations. Circumstances that benefit one dealer often benefit the whole group. But make no mistake, we all want to be the best, with the highest sales figures and top customer satisfaction ratings.

There are many different automobile manufacturers, and for each of those brands come numerous franchises. There are almost 18,000 new car dealers in the United States. Toyota alone has more than 1,700, and Volkswagen about 700. Within a 90-minute drive from my Toyota dealership in Lawrence there are nine other Toyota dealers. These numbers don't include used car dealers, or companies such as CarMax and Carvana that offer consumers a different model for buying used cars.

Today's car buyers have many choices among makes and models, new versus used, fuel vs. hybrid vs. full electric. Access to the information through the internet also has made them more informed as to what they want before they ever walk in the dealership, and if they don't like the sales pitch, they can easily go somewhere else, either in person or virtually.

In a word, competition can be intense, making it all the more important that my own intensity to meet that competition be equal to it. Even after all these years I still have the drive — that "fire in the belly" — to be the best. I like to think these are the reasons why Crown Automotive has been named "Best Place to Buy a Car" six years in a row by the readers of the *Lawrence Journal-World*, and the recipient of a Toyota President's Award 13 times in the last two decades. The latter is the highest honor a Toyota dealership can receive and is awarded to those franchises that have made a commitment to maintaining the company's high standards for customer satisfaction. People know that at

Crown Automotive they will be taken care of and have a good experience. We aim to exceed customers' expectations.

People fear the proverbial downward spiral, but the effects of intensity on any profession, side business, or hobby can in fact be the beginning of an upward spiral, intensity and consequent success increasing in tandem as you climb ever to new heights.

TENACITY

Tenacity is embodied by perseverance, resolve, and a strong will. Tenacity is finding a way to succeed — often against the odds. It's great to have smart people on your team, but intelligence means little unless an individual has the steadfast determination to get things done. What impresses me when I assess my employees' performance is not just that they reach their goals but also how they achieve them.

When one of my department heads comes to me and says they need to increase staff or make an equipment purchase, they need to prove to me that it will generate revenue. My first questions to them try to root out this justification: Is this expenditure going to translate into an increase in our bottom line, and is this really a need or simply a want? So, for example, if the request is to replace or upgrade an existing piece of equipment, such as a hoist in the service department or a paint booth in the body shop, what is the payback of the new purchase versus keeping the old apparatus that's already paid for? I tell them to put together a proposal that shows how their perceived need will help make us money, and then come see me again.

I suppose to some this might look like procrastination in my decision-making. And my old manager and mentor, Frank Stinson, told me the two things I had to do were to not procrastinate and to make quicker decisions. However, there's good reason to slow the process down and delay a bit in this type of discussion with department heads. I'm putting off the decision, not just because there may be money involved, but I also want to get a feel for the employee's tenacity. Their response gives me a window into their psyche and how strongly they feel about their request. If they make a concerted effort to get back to me and say, "this is what I want to do and these are the reasons why," then I usually approve it. But if they don't come back to me with a proposal, or if they can't show their proposed purchase is going to make us money, then I know it's not important enough to ignite their tenacity.

I've had some moments in my career when my own tenacity has served me well. During my early years with Van Chevrolet, my goal was to run my own dealership, and I was determined to make that happen at a young age. When I took over the Chevrolet store in Decatur, I was one of the youngest dealers in the state at only 32 years old. I had a goal of making our dealerships the best in central Illinois, if not the entire state. But I was a stranger to that area, and my youth made it more of a challenge to build the agency. I had to prove myself more than I would have if I had been older and had more experience in the industry.

My strategy was to make us heavily customer-centric. If we kept the customers happy, I knew we could become one of the top dealerships in the state, and if they were unhappy, I wanted to hear about it personally. Our advertising was geared toward identifying me with the dealership, so that if the customer didn't get satisfaction they were told to "ask for Miles."

I had a lot of ideas on improving all of our departments and, based on the Van Tuyl model, I wanted to give our up-and-coming people a chance to prove themselves in the business and have the same chances I'd had as future opportunities presented themselves.

I was dogged, refusing to reduce my efforts on any front, and it took some time, but the strategies paid off. We had a lot of success with the Chevrolet dealership, then purchased a Nissan franchise in 1985 and Toyota and Oldsmobile stores in 1986. My time there culminated with the awarding of the *Time* magazine Dealer of the Year award for the state.

I have also had to rely on my tenacity in markedly different circumstances. Years later, instead of being a rising young star taking over my first dealership, I was floundering. I was in search of my next career step while trying to maintain a happy family life after we moved back to Kansas City to manage a dealership that then quickly sold. I still had income coming in from the Decatur dealerships, but I wasn't ready to just quit working, and at age 44 that didn't make sense anyway.

I had already made my commitment to Paula and my daughters that we weren't moving back to Decatur or anywhere else, and I was meeting with automotive executives all over the country in hopes of landing a franchise in the Kansas City area. But there always seemed to be some barrier to entry, or the price just wasn't right. I stuck with it, though, and eventually the Lawrence dealerships became available. This was a very difficult time, but my willingness to persevere ultimately resulted in a solution that was good for everyone, most importantly for my family.

I want tenacious people in my organization because I know they'll fight for their beliefs, and that they'll develop a passion when it's necessary to see through a task or assignment. I find that tenacious individuals more often have a long-term perspective, both for their organization and for their careers, and will put short-term priorities aside in the pursuit of higher goals. The trait of tenacity indicates that someone will do everything they can to find a way, even if that way is not readily apparent. They won't give up as the day draws to close. The sales staff will work to sell one more car; the service department will perform one more oil change; the accountants will do one more profitability analysis. Mediocrity is not acceptable to them.

And it can't be for me either. As the business owner and manager, I should be the agent of change by setting the proper example. I'm pretty much an open book with people I meet, and I'm willing to share with my staff the stories of my own failures and successes, and how being tenacious has helped me truly meet the challenges that have faced me rather than push recklessly through or around them. When we take the time to be open about our trials and tribulations, others will be open to doing the same with us. The result is that we know there's a viable solution to about any problem, and we'll maintain the effort until it's resolved.

CURIOSITY

The third part of my ITCH is curiosity, which to me means not accepting answers or circumstances without questioning. Curiosity spurs us on the investigate new experiences and new ways of doing things. When curiosity is encouraged in an organization, individuals feel that they can think without limitations — outside the proverbial box — and they develop more trust in their leaders. Employees are then more apt to suggest new initiatives since they know their questions and ideas won't be shut down. This leads to better communication, more engagement in decision-making, and a reduction in conflicts. Team members and staff are less defensive when it comes to having their work critiqued, which results in more innovation and an overall better working environment.

From the perspective of business owners and managers, they must understand that they cannot afford to seek and surround themselves with yes-men. Instead, they must actively search out the curious, whose inquiries are neither a challenge to authority nor a lack of faith in leadership, but a search for a way to do it better. If an individual's leadership can't stand up to the prospect of a curious question or two, the fault is not with the questioner but with the leader.

We need to foster curiosity on all levels — from pre-school through higher education and on into the working world. Learning is constantly evolving, and so too is the professional world, but too often people take things at face value and don't look for answers on their own. People both young and old need to do their own research on the issues of the day. No matter what their beliefs, they should seek out the truth for themselves because the majority consensus on a given topic will not always be accurate or even moral. They can't be afraid to ask "Why?" or, just as importantly, "Why not?"

Business leaders need to encourage a corporate culture where people understand how important it is to keep learning, to explore new ideas, and to look for new ways of doing things. Our brains function better when we look to attempt something new that we haven't done before. When we are young and our minds are blank slates, every idea is something we've neither seen nor heard before so being open to the new and unusual is a matter of course. This type of wide-eyed childhood innocence is captivating and endearing when we encounter it in children — little sponges soaking up knowledge. So why not maintain that outlook, that practice, throughout our lives instead of morphing into adults who are close-minded and avoid surprises?

Curiosity is also not settling for just getting the job done. To maintain the practice of being curious, we would do well to review a task when it is completed, then think about how much more can be done on top of what is already completed. Care must be taken, however, because there are certain boundaries we can't cross. I've always been curious, and eager to try new things, but growing up I never wanted to disappoint or upset my parents. In my days with the Van Tuyl group, my attitude was much the same. Cecil used to always tell us to go to the edge, but don't cross the edge. In other words, it was okay to push the envelope, as long as it was legal, moral, and ethical, but we should never cross that line. It sometimes felt like I worked with Cecil on one shoulder and the devil on the other.

Now, in some instances curiosity can cause complications, as interest to pursue a new venture may cause some consternation with one's personal life. Blind curiosity that doesn't see or count the costs involved can be as problematic as having none at all. I had this laid out neatly for me when I moved the family from Decatur to Kansas City. Cecil was a guy whose management style was geared toward arousing curiosity in his staff, and when he suggested that I move back to KC to take over the Auto Plaza, my curiosity was instantly piqued.

"Why don't you come back and take the dealership over," he said, "and we can promote your general manager in Decatur to take your place there? You can sell him stock and eventually you'll be able to buy some more deals in Kansas City."

The lights went off in my head. We had already been looking for a deal for my general manager Pat Dawson to take over, and I was immediately emboldened by the confidence that Cecil had in me to run the Auto Plaza and also the suggestion that there were even more possibilities for expansion in the future. I was desperate to discuss this new opportunity with Paula, but I was already doing an analysis in my head of the pros and cons and how it would affect my wife and my 12- and 14-year-old daughters. All I could see were the positives. While the girls were six months and two years old when we originally left there, we still had families and friends all around Kansas City. There were cultural and educational possibilities for the girls that they didn't have in Decatur. And if Cecil had that much confidence in me there had to be more upside for my career in a bigger market. I was starry-eyed.

My family was much less so. At one point in my persuasive efforts, I even took the family on a flying tour over Kansas City to show them the sites and where we could live and work, but when we flew back they made it clear that they didn't want to move. I was never able to sell them on it, but my curiosity for what was possible in my professional future had already made the choice, so I made an executive decision for our family, and they arrived in Kansas City out of patience and in tears.

I have always wondered if maybe I was too curious about exploring a new frontier at that time. Certainly, my unilateral decision caused pain, heartache, and hardship for the people I loved most — difficulties that took a long time to work out. And that new future didn't turn out to be the smooth upward trajectory I'd imagined when I was talking with Cecil, not after that dealership was sold. I'm aware of how fortunate I was that we all eventually found new footing and managed to stick together.

Taken in the balance, the positives generated by curiosity outweigh the drawbacks, for a sense of wonderment is the backbone for creativity, innovation, learning and discovery. But we must do so with our eyes open, aware of the risks and how they may affect others. Curiosity is good; curiosity with a bit of wisdom thrown in is better.

HUMILITY

Everyone knows Bill Self as the head men's basketball coach at the University of Kansas, and through my support of the program and his Assists Foundation we've become friends over the years. He has built a program that consistently is among the best in the country and a perennial national title contender, winning the NCAA Championship in 2008 and 2022. In 2017 he was inducted into the Naismith Memorial Basketball Hall of Fame, and I have no doubt that someday he will be admitted to the National Collegiate Basketball Hall of Fame as well.

Even with all his success Bill has remained a humble guy — true to his Oklahoma and midwestern roots. As busy as he is in coaching and recruiting, he is willing to take the time to visit with friends and boosters. When he's able to join a group of us for golf, he arrives 30-45 minutes ahead of our tee time, talks to everybody, and kibitzes with the guys in the pro shop and clubhouse. Afterward when we're settling bets, he'll stick around and have a beer with us. A lot of high-profile coaches are known for extreme intensity and have little time for people outside their programs unless they need a favor. But Bill is not like that, and I think his deep-rooted humility and down-to-earth view of himself are big reasons he's had such so much success and impacted so many people.

As a coach, leader, or businessowner, humility is a prerequisite. If anyone in a leadership position thinks they already have all the answers, they are likely to experience some serious failure down the line. Leaders recognize that there are multiple areas of their organization where they are not — cannot be — fully cognizant of everything that's going on. They understand that many of the events and happenings that affect their businesses and even their personal lives happen out of sight.

Professionally, humility manifests in hiring people that you think are better or more capable than you are and not fearing them taking over. This kind of humility is built, not on an undervaluing of one's own abilities, but a healthy assessment of one's own strengths and weaknesses, neither overplaying the strengths nor trying to hide the weaknesses. That way, you're not afraid to delegate to people who know what they're doing because you're confident in your own abilities.

I try to hire people who one day hope to have my job, and I want to help them get to that level for themselves. Dale Backs was the perfect example of this kind of positive humility. He aspired to have his own dealership, but day-to-day he worked his tail off, respected his staff, provided excellent customer service, and always did what he thought was best for the organization.

For my own part, I obviously don't have the training or experience to overhaul an engine, nor for that matter am I fully up to speed with the latest laws and regulations in the field of human resources. I can do my homework and maybe acquire some familiarity, but I rely on others to execute. I trust my teammates to do their jobs and provide me with input on how to run the business. The most intelligent thing I can do is to know my limitations, surround myself with people who are smarter than I am, and encourage them to offer solutions to problems and suggest change. A leader who lacks humility likely won't take the same approach.

Humility keeps a leader's mind open to differing viewpoints, which contribute to the sharing of ideas and collaborative efforts that make organizations cohesive and functioning. It also allows the company to address problems more efficiently, by empowering employees to recognize difficult situations and immediately get to the core of the difficulty, without meandering their way through a bureaucratic hierarchy.

A lack of humility, on the other hand, can make a leader a control freak. They don't think anyone else can see a task through without their supervision. Workers become tentative and even afraid to make decisions or propose ideas. The result is an inefficient workforce.

Humility in a leader sets a tone for the entire organization and builds connections and relationships throughout it. When mistakes are made, humble managers are willing to share in the blame. When things go well, they are equally willing to give credit to those who are deserving. Humility allows you to celebrate rather than be skeptical of the strengths of your staff. You push them forward instead of holding them back.

Humility makes for better employees as well as better managers. I've noticed more often in recent years that when I interview someone just out of college, they seem to want to start out on top, and that's just not reality. I appreciate my parents giving me an upbringing that included the word "no" and a basic understanding of the value of hard work and paying some dues. They made sure I didn't develop a sense of entitlement — the antithesis of humility.

As a young salesman, I was also smart enough to know what I didn't know. I looked at those around me who were experienced and successful and tried to take a little something from each of them to improve my skills. But I also made sure I wasn't afraid to ask for help when I needed it. Part of what got me established in those early days was developing a broad referral network by asking friends, family, and anybody I crossed paths with to send me business. I was humble enough that I knew I needed the help of my whole community, and that I couldn't do it by myself.

As much as we each may wish to be superhuman, none of us are. But recognizing and accepting those times or situations in which we need help or the expertise of others doesn't detract from the skills and abilities that we do have. I really am passionate about allowing people to help me, and, more importantly, allowing God to help me. Humility makes both of those things work.

• • • •

Though not everyone has the same desire I do to be constantly challenged, most people still have something they want to accomplish in life — that "itch" we all want to scratch. Intensity, tenacity, curiosity, and humility can embody and apply to a wide range of human behaviors, and it's up to each of to incorporate them into our own individual situations, our individual temperaments. The beauty of developing these traits is that they have the capacity to enhance the experience of life itself, whatever our endeavors, whatever our passions, whatever our careers. Individually, they can make us more successful or more effective at our work or activities. As a group they make us more open to the world, to people, to new experiences, and more likely to engage in positive ways with the world that we find. In short, they make us better human beings.

Chapter 12
ILLUSTRIOUS

Principle #12: Be a person of achievement

*"The way to get started is to quit
talking and begin doing."*
Walt Disney

I learned to work hard because I watched my dad work hard. It seemed to me as a kid that he was behind that pharmacy counter 24 hours a day. He wouldn't even take lunch breaks. He'd bring his lunch to work and sit behind the counter and eat it while he was filling prescriptions.

I didn't comprehend his work ethic until I became an adult, responsible for myself and others. When I was a kid participating in sports, I had coaches telling me what to do to be a good ballplayer. They'd tell me when to practice, when to hit the workout room, and what skills I needed to work on. When I was going to school, my mom was there to get me out of bed on time and send me on my way (even if she couldn't convince me to listen to my teachers). In the Army, the officers made sure

I was where I needed to be when I was supposed to be there. But when we become adults and enter the working world, when we're responsible for a spouse and children, we're on our own, and the motivation to achieve must come from within. Mom was not there anymore to make sure I got up in the morning, but I still heard her voice and remembered the examples of Dad, my coaches, and a host of others pushing me forward each day to try to achieve more.

Achievement for me means reaching my goals in a combination of areas: entrepreneurial success, philanthropic and civic commitments, personal health, and financial stability. The level of success is directly proportional to the amount of personal satisfaction I receive from accomplishing the endeavor. These goals can be reached on my own or in a group setting, but the common denominator is the intrinsic and emotional reward of satisfaction I feel.

I've been lucky, but it was not always luck that made me successful. A lot of it has been persistence. I've mentioned that when I was coming up through the ranks I wanted to stand out — to be the first person my bosses would think of for a promotion. Or if the company needed someone to represent it at a meeting or civic function, I wanted to be the one chosen. I made a point to always wear a suit and tie. I learned from Cecil that if you look sharp, chances are better that you are sharp, and that creates a perception that you know what you're doing. Then it would be up to me to show that the perception could be backed up by the reality. Trying to distinguish myself, standing out among the crowd, being the best at what I do, and working hard to get there has always made sense to me as a basic method for living.

And I think it has helped me to be in a field where so much competition exists — competition can be a great motivator in the path to achievement and it certainly was for me. When I was in partnership with Cecil Van Tuyl, he would offer incentives to the partners based on the best performances. Early on in my time in Decatur, we had a "fast start" contest among the partners for $25,000, to be awarded based on who had the best first quarter of the year. And for the most net profit for the entire year Cecil was going to pay the winner $100,000. When he announced the contest, he brought $125,000 to the partner meeting and set it in front of us on a table — in cash! It was something to see that amount of money in fifty- and one-hundred-dollar bills all in one place. Needless to say, it was highly motivating.

There were probably 10 of us in the running, and I was determined. At the end of the first quarter, I was feeling pretty good about our chances which turned out to be justified — I snagged the $25,000 prize for the performance of my Decatur dealerships. If anything, the win further fueled my desire further to also have the most profitable year. It took a lot of work, but at the end of the year, I had won that too!

It was early on in my career with the dealerships in the 1980s, and I was still a fair-haired boy in the company. Mike Stewart, who was a finance and insurance consultant for the Van Tuyl organization then and still works with me as an independent broker, once told me that when I was awarded the money at a partner meeting (fortunately in the form of a check rather than cash) he could see the pride in Cecil's face. Mike waited to tell me this years later — how pleased Cecil looked in handing me the check among all the other dealers who had more experience and been around longer than I had. I wish he'd told me then. Making Cecil proud was as much a prize as the money.

In that moment, I was just overwhelmed that doing what I was supposed to do had helped me achieve something special.

What makes me most proud of this and my other business accomplishments is that I conducted myself in the right way. As Cecil said, we could go to the edge, but we couldn't cross it. And I never crossed that edge. I could have made a lot more money in my career if I had crossed that ethical edge, but I wouldn't have been able to sleep at night if I had. Car dealers historically have not rated high on the credibility scale (just above ambulance-chasing lawyers), but I was determined to take a different approach and make sure my achievements were honorable — things I could genuinely and completely be proud of.

I was not always part of the majority in that. In 1978, Chevrolet produced a Limited Edition Corvette with a black over silver paint job. It was created to serve as the official pace car of the Indianapolis 500 and was one of the hottest and most sought-after cars ever made. Many dealers were charging — and getting — a lot of money over the list price for those cars at the time, but when the buyers tried to resell them or trade them in a few years later they couldn't get back close to what they had invested. It caused some bad feelings toward those dealers who'd sought a quick extra buck.

Similarly, during the pandemic I took a call from a friend out-of-state who was looking for a new car and wanted to know how much I was asking over the sticker price. Since the semiconductor shortage had slowed the production of new automobiles, there were dealers who were doing additional markups above sticker. To me, that's not right, and down the road that type of business practice will come back to haunt you. If I sell a car for well over sticker, I may make an additional short-term profit of $5,000 or $10,000, but, down the road, when that buyer is stuck with a car that is not worth near what they paid for it, they'll be disgruntled, and justifiably so. No strong customer relationship, no repeat business, no good word-of-mouth. Achievement that undermines itself or hurts others is no achievement at all.

• • • •

I have an inherent desire to be an achiever. In just about every endeavor I've pursued in my adult life, I want my accomplishments to be of significance, as I've indicated with my desire to be an active member on boards for which I serve. I try to master skills to the best of my ability, whether it be in my golf game, the piano lessons I took as an adult, my personal training, or my attempt at running a marathon. I set high standards for myself and am not satisfied if I don't reach them.

But in order to be satisfied with myself, I don't need personal recognition of my achievements, which may sound odd, given that I have received some acknowledgement and am proud of it. I don't campaign for awards, though, nor do I participate in civic functions so that I can get my name in the paper or on a website. Most of what I do and achieve is out of the public eye. My intrinsic motivation and the goals I set for myself have always been the strongest force driving forward my achievement, and the occasional byproduct has been that others have noticed, often in gratifying ways.

Though my dealerships have often been award-winning among franchises and within industry associations, those are generally based on specific measures of customer satisfaction with sales and service. There have been a couple honors, however, that came as a surprise and were much more about me as a person. These are the ones that stick with me most and continually make me want to live up to how others view me.

In 2015, I was awarded the Meritorious Achievement Award by the Pittsburg State Alumni Association. Established in 1958, this is the Alumni Association's highest award based on career achievement and takes into consideration a person's participation and leadership in civic and professional organizations. Since three of our family members — Paula, Mandi, and I — are Pitt State graduates, I have always supported the school monetarily. But this award came several years before our family made a large donation for maintenance and improvements to the indoor basketball and volleyball arena, so it didn't just feel like a quid pro quo situation. For someone who struggled academically and feels genuine affection toward his alma mater, to be recognized in such a way was very meaningful. Just as I have long been grateful for the place in my life held by Pitt State, it felt like the university valued me for being part of its legacy.

The other honor that continues to mean so much to me came through the Kansas chapter of Junior Achievement. JA is an organization that's been around more than a century and is dedicated to educating young people about entrepreneurship, career readiness, and financial literacy. Business leaders volunteer their time to help students in grades K-12 plan for their futures by making smart academic and economic decisions. The Kansas chapter of Junior Achievement is a strong one, reaching about 28,000 students statewide each year. It also serves as the curator for the Lawrence Business Hall of Fame, which inducts four local business leaders each February. In 2017, I was honored to be named one of their laureates.

The stated criteria for induction into the Hall of Fame were business excellence, entrepreneurial spirit, courageous thinking, inspiring leadership, community impact, the ability to serve as a role model, and enduring accomplishments. I had always assumed that one also had to be a significant donor to Junior Achievement, and I hadn't been up to that point. And it was only after I was named to the Hall of Fame that one of my employees, Connie Beebe, began to volunteer for them. To be judged worthy by those standards alone was quite humbling, and I was surprised when I got the call that I was going to be inducted. I sure support JA now.

It was a very special occasion. At the ceremony, I had a chance to speak along with the other inductees and was introduced by then 11-year-old Mavrick Hawkins. Mav participated in Junior Achievement, and I had known his father, Jeff, for many years through basketball. Jeff Hawkins played at Kansas in the mid-2000s under both Roy Williams and Bill Self and is currently the head boys' basketball coach at Pembroke Hill School in Kansas City. Though I'd known the family for a long time, after Mav's flattering introduction of me, we became very close. I was so touched by Mav's comments that I was already choking up even before I reached the podium. Following his words, a video was played showing pictures of me with friends and family and testimonials from lifelong friends and business associates. At that point, it was hard for me to even start my speech.

I've already shared that my father maintained a tough guy exterior. On the inside, however, he was very sensitive. Mention anything about family, and his eyes would immediately well up. People didn't expect that out of him, but it happened all the time, including when he gave a toast at my wedding. I don't pretend to be as stoic nor as outwardly tough as he was, but I'm every bit as emotional. If I talk about my family, or about one of my employees who has succeeded at something, my voice will start to crack, and I'll get choked up.

So, there I was, being honored in front of several hundred people, trying not to bawl. But I managed to get going, and I opened with thank yous and recognition for my wife, my daughters, my grandson, my sister, and friends who were in attendance. I talked about my parents and the good examples they set for me.

At that point, I told them that if I were smart, I would just say thank you and sit down. But I love having a microphone in my hand, so I continued, and I talked about how flattered and humbled I was to join the other inductees that night, as well as the past laureates. By this point, my handkerchief was getting a heck of a workout.

As I told the audience, when we talk about a hall of fame in athletics, it's a marker of career achievement based on statistics and championships to which everyone aspires. But in the business world you're mainly focused on finding someone to buy your products and services, and how best to maximize revenue. By definition, a hall of fame is a special place that honors teams or individuals who have done something illustrious in their career. They are well known, respected, and admired for past accomplishments.

"Now I have been called a lot of things," I said from the podium, "but illustrious has never been one of them." The audience smiled kindly back at me, but I meant it. It was so great to be recognized for my years in business in Lawrence, but as I spoke, I was even more reflective on the many blessings I have received from above. I told of how inspired I was by the people I met every day, and how I tried to learn something new every day as well. I shared my philosophy that everyone in my organization was of equal importance, from the pre-wash guys in the service department up to the general manager, and to me as the owner.

I told the audience that evening what amounts to my philosophy of true achievement and how we get there, which

I thought was particularly relevant to the efforts and goals of our Junior Achievement sponsors. Indeed, working to raise our children to be high achievers should be important to us all.

Obviously, parents want to make sure their children are safe and secure and to keep them out of the deep end of the pool. But it is the reality of life that they will end up in the deep water, regardless of how careful we may be. It's precisely in those moments that our children need to have the tools to make the right choices, to know how to survive and even thrive, to become people of achievement. This is a big question that I've always asked myself: Do we provide our next generation with the right values and morals and courage to make the right choices when the going gets tough? In other words, can we teach our children how to swim, even when they're in the deep end?

Today in many families we have the helicopter parents who are afraid to let their children face failure in any academic or athletic endeavor. The educational system is also sometimes at fault for allowing students to move on even if their performance is not satisfactory. This tends to result in feelings of entitlement, rather than a practice of achievement through self-motivation and hard work. This sense of entitlement could be a reason that many young adults handle the stress of disappointment poorly. They lose focus and can't deal with the slightest setback because their attention is on a perceived (but inaccurate) threat to survival, not achievement.

My personal journey began when I was born into my family with the parents I had. They gave me everything they could to help me flourish, and they also set the boundaries for me so that I knew what was right. I attended public school, and though I didn't distinguish myself academically, my parents supplemented my education by sending me to Hebrew school, which proved to be great leadership training for me. We had a youth group in the synagogue, and I stepped up to lead our junior congregation on Saturday mornings before we would go into main sanctuary, where we'd read the Torah and listen to the reflections of the rabbi. I learned early not to be afraid to lead, even in a small group.

My parents set a great example for me as well. My dad received a lot of awards from the synagogue, including Father of the Year, and Mom was once named Mother of the Year. Growing up like we did, my sisters and I were taught to be God-fearing, which gave us a conscience. I did some silly things — my friends and I egged one classmate's house and threw pumpkins on the porch of another during high school, both of which resulted in some discipline and heavy clean-up duty. But for the most part I stayed out of trouble. My peers and I didn't take drugs or carry guns or do other things that would have had life-changing consequences.

When I look back on my 75 years, I don't see myself as being any more special than anyone else, much less that I should be christened with the adjective of "illustrious." But I was given so many opportunities and had so many good things happen to me. I was definitely helped by a lot of people in my quest to be a person of achievement. I want to see the same for the generations to come.

I grew up around and became friends with a lot of people who became high achievers — business owners and civic leaders, top-flight coaches and college administrators, leaders of successful charities and religious organizations. I've noticed come common threads among them. They usually come from families in which the parents supported their activities but also encouraged them to be independent and free-thinking. Building a thriving business or making the community better has been more important to them than material or monetary gains, and while many achieved financial rewards, those are a barometer of success rather than the ultimate goals.

They are continually on the move and taking action, not prone to procrastination, and not afraid to confront their fears. They like being around people, with their lives centered on their own relationships. These achievers also take greater satisfaction from achieving their aim rather than receiving recognition. And finally, and most importantly, they are honest, with a clear set of values and a lifestyle consistent with those values.

When you're doing things the right way and giving your share and a little more, I guess you will win some awards, and if those organizations think I'm worthy, I'm happy about it. Every once in a while, though, I will indulge myself privately and reflect upon my achievements — and I do take some pride that I have reached some level of success. I have quite a collection of memorabilia in my office (Paula says I never throw anything away, and she's right — as usual.) It's nice to sit back in my chair and look at the pictures, the plaques, and the autographed items sent to me by people I've met over the decades — and remember the people and events I've had the pleasure to know and experience. I realize that I've achieved more than I ever thought possible, and that a lot of folks were there to help me, many of whom are gone now. I wish I could tell them thanks one more time.

LUNCH WITH LOU

Anyone who has even the slightest knowledge about college football is familiar with the accomplishments of Lou Holtz. In 33 seasons as a head coach at six different institutions, he compiled a glittering record of 249-132-7. His most notable accomplishments came at Notre Dame, where he went 100-30-2 in 11 seasons and saw his team voted as the 1988 national champions with an undefeated 12-0 record — the last national title that the Irish have won. In 2008 Notre Dame unveiled a statue of Lou with his record engraved along with the words "Trust, Love, Commitment." He is the only coach ever to take six different schools to bowl games as well as the only one to lead four different programs to Top 20 finishes in the final national polls.

After he retired from coaching, he joined the broadcasting crews at CBS and later ESPN. He has been inducted into the College Football Hall of Fame and has been awarded a Presidential Medal of Freedom. Lou also has authored or contributed to 10 books — some on football but others on developing a game plan for life. It's been an illustrious career indeed.

A few years back, we were fortunate that our Lawrence dealership had once again received the Toyota Presidents Award, and Paula and I traveled to Florida for the ceremony, where Lou would be the keynote speaker.

As I was on the National Dealer Council for Toyota, I was privileged to be invited to join Lou for lunch. It also helped that I was known to have a strong interest in sports, so the organizers knew it would be easy for us to find things to talk about. Years before, when I had an Oldsmobile dealership, I had heard him speak at one of their conventions, so I talked a little about that and how much I thought about him as a speaker and motivator. A common theme in his speeches is how a little guy with a speech impediment could win a national championship in football, along with becoming an author, broadcaster, and recipient of a Presidential Medal of Freedom. I've always loved watching and listening to him.

My discussion during that lunch with Lou went well beyond the past speeches and playing fields. We talked about our families and life in general. We had our pictures taken together and I gave him my business card. I told him how much I appreciated him and thanked him for being at the event.

Paula and I arrived early to the reception that night and noticed Lou was standing by himself. We went over and started talking with him and truly began to develop a nice relationship. He thanked me for giving him my business card earlier and said that he had something he wanted to send me.

A few weeks passed and I basically had put our exchange in the back of my mind, when a package arrived for me. Inside was a Notre Dame football with the handwritten inscription:

Miles E. Schnaer — Congratulations,
you not only perform like a champion
every day, but you also live like one.
Lou Holtz

Lou is talked about a lot — in both good and bad ways. He's always been known to speak his mind, and while that has occasionally resulted in controversy, he has remained a much sought-after public speaker. He has a self-deprecating sense of humor, he's frank about his actions and choices, and he's a pretty spiritual guy who is sincere about his beliefs. And you couldn't ask for a more fun and colorful person to be around — it certainly pulled me in. His thoughtfulness in following up with the autographed football was an unexpected bonus I still appreciate.

Chapter 13
HIT YOUR HIGH BEAMS

Principle #13: Lead by shining
the brightest light to create a
positive company culture

*"The greatest leader is not necessarily the one
who does the greatest things. He is the one that
gets the people to do the greatest things."*
Ronald Reagan

In the Jewish faith, we celebrate Hanukkah in late November or sometime in December, about the same time that Christians observe the Christmas season. Also known as the Festival of Lights, Hanukkah commemorates the recovery of Jerusalem and the rededication of the temple in the second century B.C. The best-known symbol of this season is the menorah, with its eight candles kept lit throughout the eight days and eight nights of the festival. It is a very special time in our faith, one that gives shape to the symbolic power of light.

I've personally received the light of inspiration over the last

15 years from my association with Rabbi Zalman Tiechtel who, along with his wife, Nechama, directs the Chabad Jewish Student Center on the campus of the University of Kansas. The Tiechtels arrived in Lawrence in 2006, looking to increase engagement and involvement among the Jewish students, and to be a conduit to connect those students with the university and Lawrence communities. They have been extremely successful, building a new center and now serving hundreds of students who come to KU from across the country.

They knew hardly a soul when they arrived, but Zalman made a connection with another Chabad rabbi who had bought several cars from Crown and suggested that the Tiechtels come and see me. As complete strangers, they showed up at the reception desk and asked for me. After I came to the showroom and introduced myself, our connection was immediate, and we must have talked for an hour. I told them that if there was anything I could ever do for them not to hesitate to give me a call. I could tell they sincerely appreciated it, and since that time Rabbi Tiechtel has become a friend and a spiritual advisor — and even occasionally a customer. I donate money to the Chabad Center, and Crown Automotive also sponsors their annual calendar, which is the only true Jewish calendar in the state of Kansas. My picture is on the back with the greeting, "From your fellow Jewhawk," which always makes me smile.

When we part after our meetings, Rabbi Tiechtel often tells me that he feels better than when he first walked in the door. He expresses his gratitude that I have shared my time, though I should really be the more thankful one that he's shared his time with me. I'm able to talk to him in a way that I couldn't with anyone else, and the high esteem in which I hold him makes his kind words that much more moving. In the midst of my search for spiritual leadership and guidance, he says he finds himself inspired by how I conduct myself on a daily basis. It's a humbling and important reminder for me that, both in business and in the community, I should be an example for others. My own light has the capacity to shine and influence others for good.

I hope I'm seen in this way by my employees. As someone running a business, it is important that my personal light is seen, and a positive ethic is absorbed by those who work in my organization. Great leaders illuminate and create future leaders, and I have long aspired to be a great leader. Certainly, to have a great organization the top level of management must build a culture that fosters and encourages the development of even more great leaders. As such, a leadership culture needs to be systemic and pervasive throughout the entire organization. Managers need to lead by example — taking care of themselves, supporting healthy lifestyle habits, and encouraging employees to have fulfilling lives outside of work.

True leaders also need to exhibit a sense of confidence. They often have faith in a higher power which can ground their moral code. And, without fail, they have a belief in themselves to succeed as an individual and as a leader of an organization. Nobody wants to follow somebody who is mealy-mouthed or doesn't look like they're confident in what they're doing. If a person doesn't even believe in their own plan or goal, they will be hard-pressed to get anyone else to.

For myself, my ultimate goal is to build a culture, not just a company. When an employee joins the Crown family, we make sure they receive a proper welcome and orientation to our team values, and they receive a copy of our employee handbook which includes a letter from me detailing my background in the business, commitment to excellence, and the hope that they will become a valuable part of our team and vision. It concludes with our mission statement:

> We, the employees of Crown Toyota and Volkswagen, and our families are dedicated to:
> - Superior customer service in all phases of our operation.
> - Excellence in all actions.
> - Dignity and respect for individuals.
> - Mutual support in the attainment of common goals.
> - Pride in the facility through a program of cleanliness and orderliness.
> - Community awareness and support.
>
> These beliefs serve as a foundation for the traditions, growth, and success of our organization.

What stands out in that mission statement — what I made sure would stand out — is the focus on people. With the exception of the reference to Toyota and Volkswagen, you wouldn't even know that we are in the automotive business. And we're really not — we're in the people business.

In fact, for the sake of their employees, every business should view itself as being in the people business. And people at their core share some common essentials, whatever the business may be. They want to be recognized and made to feel like they are contributing. They want to understand the mission of their organization and their importance in contributing to it. In the long run, they want more than to just collect a paycheck. I can't control the actions of others, but I can control the message I send and the influence I have over our team, and if I do that right I will get the collective buy-in. By my daily actions I can create the proper environment so that the sense of our mission is shared.

This also means shining the high beam on new opportunities, so that they are recognizable not only to upper management but to the entire staff. If an organization holds too tightly to old practices and procedures without allowing for what new light may illuminate, then it may become stagnant, and possibly irrelevant. I look at how the automobile sales model has evolved over my 50 years in the business, from the days when most prospects walked into the showroom with limited knowledge, to today, when the consumer can access unlimited information as to a car's features and price — so much so that they often know as much as the salesperson. Sales tactics that succeeded in decades past are ineffective and obsolete today.

Our service departments also operate much differently than they did in the past. Cars today are like computers on wheels, and those who work on the repair side are highly trained technicians who must be familiar with a wide range of engine types, not to mention such modern tech features as 360-degree camera parking, forward collision warning, and lane keeping assist. As the products have become more high-tech and sophisticated, so have the consumers. They read, they study, they compare, and we must be ready to address their questions and concerns. We need to make sure our employees are proficient in all aspects of their job.

I can't personally train all 110 people in my organization on the latest industry trends, but I can damn sure install department heads who share my management style and are open to the exploration of new and better ways to run the business. Even with all the changes in the world in general and in the automobile industry in particular, some basic tenets have stayed true throughout the years. This trickle-down influence ensures that we maintain the unchanging values of keeping people first and of skill development and innovation.

Some leaders obsess over fixing problems, and that can also be a detriment to progress. Serious flaws in any organization must certainly be addressed, but picking apart every little issue can distract us from the big picture — the revelations of the possibilities ahead. And everybody needs to be involved in identifying and solving problems within the organization, not just the owner or manager. The best leaders empower their staff with this authority. You shouldn't have to ask permission to take responsibility or show concern.

Anyone can be given a leadership title or position, but history shows a lot of errors have been made in business, in politics, and in the military by picking the wrong person. Leadership is much more about influence than a title. A true leader figures out a way to be innovative and inspirational, but also exhibits exemplary behavior. Otherwise, their attempts at inspiration lack any real power or energy, and they can be seen as hypocritical to the members of their team. It is about being a force for good and making others feel important. People need attention on a consistent basis, not just periodically. When you speak, speak to them, not at them.

This is also why I make a point of being accessible to our employees. As I said earlier, it's a good habit to be in the right place at the wrong time, to be wandering around to check and see what's going on — not only to observe and correct but to encourage. When one of my salespeople has had trouble closing deals, I visit with them. I let them know that I started out selling cars, and I know exactly what it's like to go through a day or week without a sale and feel the pressure. I know it's hard to catch up toward meeting your goals, and keeping yourself going can be a struggle. Whatever the demands of the business, we have common ground.

That's why I walk around and talk to the staff and get to know them, and I ask my department heads to keep me informed on major events in the lives of their staff members. And that encourages me to stay involved, too. When something has happened to someone personally — a death in the family, a tough medical diagnosis, a marriage, a graduation, a new baby — I'll seek out that individual and pay my respects or offer congratulations. In most cases I can relate since I've probably experienced the same pain or joy sometime in my life. I hope it gives them a little inspiration to know that those of us in upper management care and can understand how they feel.

I also have an open-door policy with all my employees. I want them to know that if there's an issue they can't resolve with their department head, they are welcome to come to me. With our culture we have few issues with labor relations or discrimination, so normally it's a simple concern. I do want them to go through the proper channels first, and my managers know that they need to try to handle it first and are empowered to do so, but it's important to me that no one ever feels stuck or unheard, that everyone knows the owner is cognizant of their needs and is available to meet.

I also foster a strong company culture in the hope that people feel valued by avoiding cookie-cutter expectations for all employees or all departments. If you give everyone the same goals and incentives, you're making a mistake. As an example, our incentive and bonus programs are structured to fit the individual. We have incentives to reward the top producers, but we also have incentives so that the average or new producers can still earn a bonus. And we don't limit our incentives to just the people selling cars. The service department employees have volume goals for sales of items such as tires and batteries or for working with customers to stick to their recommended maintenance schedules. The finance department employees can earn extra through the sale of extended warranties or other items to protect the car. In all these goals, our staff is instructed to sell these items based on the value to the customer — not to themselves. Would they buy it themselves? Would they sell it to their mother? I make it clear that I never want to hear that a customer didn't realize what they were buying and were taken advantage of.

I expect our staff to work hard but I also like to make our workplace fun. Allowing the workplace to be joyless is no way to shine a light or influence the organizational culture. To help encourage a positive atmosphere, we'll have a couple of employee parties each year, and sometimes even set up a little surprise. Something as simple as a visit from the ice cream man bringing free popsicles on a hot summer day can boost morale. I just like to show I care enough to take an interest even in small things, even in the enjoyment of the day.

I've been asked how I've had such low staff turnover through the years, and frankly it's because our people make pretty good money. The potential is there for them to make more than they would at other dealerships. I give them an opportunity to share in the success of the company, and the last five years or so have been particularly good to us.

By contrast, some dealerships will put caps on the amount their managers can earn through incentives, but I've always tried to share the profits with the people who do the job. If they succeed in surpassing their goals then I also do better, so I don't change pay and incentive plans to keep more rewards for myself. If you set those percentages right and employees figure out a way to make it work and they exceed expectations, I don't cut them back because they're making too much money. The longer they stay the higher their bonus levels are, as well as the percentage contributed to those retirement accounts. This encourages people to want to stay and retire with us.

In recent years I've also given my general managers shares in the company stock. I did that with the late Dale Backs when he moved to Lawrence, as Cecil Van Tuyl did for me when I went to Decatur. It was a boost to me then, and it's a great incentive for my guys now.

If a leader can get his team to believe in what he is telling them, and they know that he cares about them, they'll realize that everyone will be successful. I've tried to do that by letting everybody in my organization, from the kids who wash the cars to the general managers, know that every cog helps turn the wheel. Everybody is part of the team, and we will all succeed together. If I can shine the light properly, it shines on us all.

· · · ·

People have asked me whose leadership styles I have emulated. Because I'm a fan, I like to look at the sports world and pick out a variety of successful leadership skills among coaches. Prominent in inspiring me and others was the late Dick Nagy, the former Illinois assistant coach and my close friend from my days in Decatur. He was part of a highly successful program at Illinois for 17 years and had his share of accomplishments at the junior college level. Dick was a solid leader and could be intense in his coaching, but he was also a person you could talk with about life. He was a good listener no matter what the topic. He was also a strong man of faith, and even though he was Christian and I was Jewish, we shared belief in a common God. Even though he has left us, I feel his light still shines on me today and influences the light I try to shine for others.

And I've already talked about Bill Self, a two-time NCAA basketball champion at Kansas, and his influence on me. He has a knack for making his players understand what their roles are, what they can do to not only succeed but even exceed what they thought was possible. He may be demanding at times, but that refusal to settle for second-best is backed up with instruction and support so that people can rise to the next level. And the true team player takes those instructions and works to improve because they know they're contributing to the success of the team. Then there's also Lou Holtz, the national champion college football coaching legend. His philosophy of coaching revolved around three key principles that resonate with me daily: trust, commitment, and care.

I've had lots of leaders directly light the way for me in my business, too. I've mentioned mentors such as Cecil Van Tuyl, Frank Stinson, and Ron Huber, who each taught me something about the business in their own style. Another guy I credit with coaching me a lot as a young salesman is Jerry Dahmer. He was the general manager of Van Chevrolet when I first started there, and later became the successful owner of Cable-Dahmer Chevrolet. Jerry really knew the business and passed down a lot of expertise. And he was one of the best at leading us, teaching us all how to make it work.

Someone whose leadership style I've gotten to know and admire outside of my business is Gene Bicknell, who became the largest Pizza Hut franchisee before selling his interests in 2006. A fellow Pitt State graduate, he also founded and sold a plastics company and has served on the boards of banks and major corporations. He's run for political office, raised millions of dollars for not-for-profits (including Pitt State), acted in movies, and authored a couple of books — the most recent at the age of 89. It's quite a résumé for the consummate self-made man who was born in Picher, Oklahoma, to a miner with an eighth-grade education.

Even with all his accomplishments and his connections in the corporate world and show business, when you're with Gene, he makes you feel like the most important person in the world. One time, we were dining together and his phone rang. I could see that the name on the caller ID was "Bobby Vinton," the singer and actor who was one of the biggest teen idols of the 1960s. From 1962 through '72, Vinton had more number one hits than any other male vocalist, including Elvis! Gene quietly hit the red decline button on his phone and continued our conversation.

"I'll call him back later," Gene said without any pretense. A lot of people would be inclined to make a big production of "who they know," but Gene isn't like that at all. He was more interested in talking with me than a superstar. I couldn't have felt more valued.

• • • •

There are three tools that have been immensely beneficial to me to shine the light as a manager and make sure the positive company culture I aim for takes root: patience, recognition, and delegation.

Patience is something that I've had to develop over the years — it takes patience to become patient. When you first start out you want everything to click from day one, but success for an organization comes with a steady, managed approach. It's similar to young athletes entering the professional ranks. When they get into their first game, they find everything is moving faster than it has for them before, but with experience the pace seems to slow down. They see the developments on the field or court more clearly and learn how to adjust while the action is in progress. It's a skill that takes time to learn and time to develop. We all have to be willing to give it space to unfold.

Recognition I've already discussed in some detail, and it involves developing awareness of people as individuals and also appreciating their production by providing tangible rewards. I want my team members to know they are appreciated for who they are, and that I will give them an opportunity to make a good living. What is happening in their lives is also important to me. They know that if they need to see me, I will be available. This lets the employees know I am supportive, but also helps me recognize any festering issues before they become real problems. If I can get ahead of the situation, maybe we can talk it out while I'm in their department, rather than later behind closed doors in my office.

The ability to delegate I learned early by example, when others had faith in and delegated to me. If you really are committed to hiring people better than you, then you should have no issue giving them the proper authority and the opportunity to make money. Though sometimes I wonder if I've delegated too well. That's a byproduct of getting good people, paying them well, and creating a culture of chemistry in which everyone understands their place on the team. There are days I wonder if they even need me at all.

It's nice to feel confident that my managers will keep everything running smoothly, though they tell me they still need me around. Maybe they're just being kind, but I do think this little light has a bit more shining to do.

Chapter 14
DON'T STAY IN THE DITCH

Principle #14: Learn from adversity

*"I've learned that something constructive
comes from every defeat."*
Tom Landry

Dennis Wilson and I worked together at Van Chevrolet back in the early 1970s. He was on the new car side, and I sold used cars, but we were both young guys starting out and really bonded. He ended up owning a couple of small dealerships in the Kansas City area and was an intense businessman who cared a lot about his employees and coworkers.

Dennis eventually entered the world of politics and was elected to both the Kansas House of Representatives and the State Senate. He also served as Treasurer for Johnson County and director of the Kansas lottery, in addition to having business interests in banking and insurance. He passed away in 2020, and a stretch of U.S. Route 69 was renamed in his memory. He lived quite a life in his 70 years and clearly touched a lot of people.

I'd lost my closeness with Dennis during my years in Illinois, but when I was struggling with moving my family back to Kansas City and taking over the Auto Plaza in 1991, we reconnected. He came back into my life at a time when I was in desperate need of a good friend. He and I had a relationship like few people I've known, and he could relate to me as I was going through my struggles. He stuck with me and talked me off the proverbial ledge a few times.

His friendship meant a lot and I knew he wasn't just blowing smoke when he gave me words of encouragement or comfort. Dennis knew from personal experience how to overcome adversity. He had gone through some ups and downs in the car business, and after he was diagnosed with the blood disorder that eventually led to his death, he battled it with courage for years. Despite his setbacks, he kept a positive attitude and ultimately succeeded both in business and as an outstanding public servant. And he had the heart to help me keep going as well. I'm sure he provided the same comfort to the many others who were fortunate enough to cross his path, too.

This period in the early 1990s was a very difficult time for me. Though my reputation and pride had taken a hit with the NCAA investigation, my Decatur dealerships were still doing well. But I had left that solid situation and was moving my family, despite their repeated objections, to a new home in a different state. Even with all the positives I saw in returning to our home region, I had two daughters in their formative years who did not want to leave the only town they had ever known. Initially, Paula and the girls had stayed behind so they could finish out the school year, so I spent about three months by myself in a rented house. I drove to Kansas City alone in a parts truck containing my clothes, a bed, a dresser, a TV, a kitchen table and chairs, and a treadmill so I could try to keep in shape. It was a stark and lonely few months.

The new position at the Auto Plaza was also proving more challenging than expected, particularly when the Gulf War started and upset the oil market and world economy almost simultaneously with my first day. There were a lot of changes that I felt had to be made, as a new manager often does. The dealership was behind on accounts payable, and the place was way overstaffed. We had around 350 employees, of which we cut back about 100 in the first 30 days. Based on my experience we simply didn't need all those people. They were operating like the worst version of government — if they needed something done, they would just go out and find a new hire to do it. I had to stop that.

With all the upheaval and changes, the phones were ringing off the hook. I'd never had a secretary before. As part of my desire to be accessible I had always taken pride in the fact that I didn't have my calls screened, but I was getting 50 or 60 messages a day from upset vendors, other people wanting to sell us something, job seekers, and friends who wanted to say hi and welcome me back to Kansas City. I didn't have time to talk, or even call them back most of the time, so I moved a young woman who was in charge of inventory control to a desk outside of my office to basically become my office manager. She was able to answer the constantly ringing phone and take care of everything that didn't need my personal attention.

That worked fine, except that one time when Paula, who was still in Decatur, called and got screened. It didn't go over very well, but Paula understood when I explained, and my new office manager learned a quick lesson on who should obviously qualify as an exception to her screening method. After that I had a separate line put in my office so that Paula could call me directly.

On the outside, I purposefully gave the impression that I was doing great. We were filming commercials and placing articles in the newspapers celebrating the "hometown boy's" return to Kansas City. We put ads in the *Jewish Chronicle* to get the word out to the community and my old contacts that I was back. On the inside, however, I was feeling a real lack of confidence for the first time in my career. You always have days that don't go well and make you feel down from time to time, but this was different. This wasn't letting up. Thank goodness I had Dennis as a sounding board. He knew exactly what I was going through, trying to operate a new store, dealing with staff changes, and trying to motivate people to do things differently than they did before. And he was a kind listening ear as I worried over my family, too.

Cecil was also always supportive of me and what I was trying to do. We'd meet every Saturday morning, and I would have all my notes on a yellow pad to share with him. Sometimes we would meet after work at a local restaurant, and he'd buy me a Scotch to get me to open up. We developed a stronger relationship than we'd ever had.

About a year later, after my family had finally relocated and gotten comfortably settled in Kansas City, we had that offer to sell the Auto Plaza. I really didn't want to sell — I was just starting to feel like my feet were almost back under me. I had worked hard to make the Auto Plaza a successful operation and had made a commitment to my family to see it through. But the offer was too good to pass on, even though it hurt. I knew there were other opportunities out there, but when we met with the group that was buying us, reality hit me. When I shared the news with Paula that we might have to move again — Cecil thought there was a place in Springfield, Missouri that might fit — it wasn't good. I had made the choice on my own to leave Decatur, but this time the family was going to have a say, and they made it clear that this time they weren't going anywhere.

What followed the sale of the Auto Plaza was probably my lowest point. I was sailing by myself with only a few people to support me. I couldn't sleep much or well, so I'd go to the couch at night because I didn't want to disturb Paula. I would be up all night, and then had to find a place to conduct business because I didn't have an office anymore and trying to work at home was uncomfortable. I set up shop in Dennis Spivak's conference room to use the phone and look for deals, and for a week each month I'd head back to Decatur. I still owned those stores, and I didn't want the employees to think I was going to sell those dealerships.

The unknown was something I wasn't prepared for. Cecil still wanted me to stay with him and take over another dealership, which would likely not have been in Kansas City. But I went to him and said I was going to have to take some time to regain stability in my family life. He understood and told me to get my situation straightened out before we attempted any new venture.

Paula and I were prepared to at least get our daughters through high school, and in the end she agreed that after they graduated she would go with me anywhere I wanted to go. About that time Toyota and Chevrolet started contacting me about the dealerships in Lawrence. At first their bad reputations made me dismissive, but over time the prospect became more appealing since it would allow me to stay in the Kansas City area. I closed those purchases in 1994, and I stayed partners with Cecil in Decatur until 1997. He didn't want me to leave the organization and planned to get me back in another one of his dealerships down the line. In the back of my mind, I thought maybe someday we would put some deals together and be partners again, but it was clear that it was time for me to move on, and I'm glad I did. We reached an agreement for him to buy me out and bring in Pat Dawson as his partner in Decatur. We shook hands and remained friends, but for the first time in 25 years I was on my own professionally.

The challenges weren't over yet, however, as I started my new ventures in Lawrence. My overall good reputation as an owner and manager in Decatur, and even in my short time with the Auto Plaza, didn't translate to immediate success in my new locations, where the credibility of the previous owners had muddied the waters. Randy Habiger, now the general manager of my Toyota franchise, was just out of college working on the sales floor for the Sonny Hill Chevrolet franchise when I took over. I still remember how the sales staff looked to me like a khaki-pants fraternity. Their method had been to hire a bunch of inexperienced guys, not give them much training, and then weed out the ones who couldn't figure it out on their own. It was not a well-run operation, and the negative reputation was deserved.

We struggled, but I knew what I was doing was the right thing even though it was tough. It was a long struggle, though. It took a couple of years before I felt we had arrived.

During the hard days I remember wondering why I had made that move to Kansas City. I hadn't needed to do that. Everything was going well in Decatur. I could have put Pat Dawson into another dealership while retaining my ownership and continuing to build my business. It was easy to get deep into self-doubt and second guessing. I knew that objectively there were good reasons to come back, but it came at a cost, and I wasn't the only one who had to pay it. I was fortunate to still have the support and love of my family, rough as it was sometimes, and lucky that they stuck with me. In the end they grew to be pleased that we returned to Kansas City, and most of my professional success has come since we came back.

But success doesn't prevent trouble from rearing up again, and another difficult period for me came in the late 2000s, during the General Motors bankruptcy process that culminated in their Chapter 11 filing in 2009 — one of the largest bankruptcies in our country's history. With the intervention of the federal government, there was a subsequent restructuring and asset sale from which a new GM emerged. The company was really struggling then and riding the dealers hard, but frankly the products weren't very good. For years, American automakers had built cars that they wanted to sell, while the Japanese and other foreign manufacturers were making cars people actually wanted to buy. On my lot it was easy to see the difference. We had Chevrolets being towed in for significant service problems, while on the Toyota side customers were just driving in for routine maintenance.

GM started terminating dealerships across the country. A few years earlier they had tried to buy me out at a price that was a bit low, and in the meantime the other GM dealer in Lawrence started sending me letters with offers to buy as well. Then GM filed for bankruptcy, the other dealer's offer went away, and the value of my dealership went from about $3 million to $1 million. I eventually joined with some other dealers from across the country in filing a class-action suit against General Motors for the devaluation of our franchises. It's still pending, but I don't expect anything to come from it — it's a bit like suing the government, since the feds basically bailed out GM. Really, it's just up to me to learn what I can from what happened and move forward.

There have been other situations in my life where I was thrown a curve and had to be determined to stay the course: that NCAA inquiry at Illinois, the deceptive practices by Volkswagen on the diesel engines, various recalls and investigations like the sticky pedal situation with Toyota. Sometimes it's a hard fight to keep outside forces from kicking you off the rails.

• • • •

Cecil used to call some of the partners "rich and good-lookin.'" Those were the guys he thought were only out for the material rewards, the ones who wanted to make a lot of money, buy big houses, and join the country clubs. Those types didn't last long in the organization. Cecil hadn't grown up that way, and neither had I, so I thought I was safe from acquiring that attitude. I certainly didn't ever think I had become that way, but maybe I had without realizing it. I may have thought I was bulletproof, but when I came back to Kansas City and the Auto Plaza, I was brought to my knees pretty quickly.

We can learn a lot from adversity. I know I sure did. It is ingrained in us from an early age that failure is bad, and that mistakes are to be avoided. But failure and mistakes are often the result of a new experiment and can be used as a learning opportunity. We didn't successfully ride a bike or hit a fastball the first time we tried it. When we took our first music lessons, we often hit the wrong key or played a sour note. But that can't cause us to lay down the bike, the bat, or the instrument and never touch it again.

I've had my trials, but for the most part they've been very manageable. I learned that God doesn't put more on your plate than you can handle, although there was a time when I felt my plate was the size of those trays you get at the all-you-can-eat buffet. In the long run the experiences made me better. Your life changes, one way or another, as you go through adversity, and mine certainly made me a better husband and father and an overall better person.

To counteract adversity, it is important to develop resilience. It's not a trait we're born with — it's developed over time by facing and ultimately overcoming adversity. You have to focus on what you can control and make the best of it. The resilient ones take charge of their situations, seize the moment, and choose to move on. They work on their relationships and identify new opportunities. They find strength in their religious and spiritual lives.

If you face adversity, whether in your personal or professional life, in the form of a health scare for you or your family, or a negative financial situation, there are ways to manage and come out of it even better than you were before.

First, don't be afraid to confide in someone or to ask for help. You're not a weak person if you rely on others for assistance and counsel. You're not out there alone, and there are plenty of people inside and even outside your inner circle who are more than willing to offer a helping hand. I had to seek a professional during my lowest period, but if that is not a feasible option, look to your rabbi, minister, or priest to share your feelings. I visit regularly with Rabbi Tiechtel — at least twice a month in person or by phone, even when I'm at my home in Florida. He reinforces for me that it's the spiritual rather than the material gifts that are most important.

There may also be a friend or relative who will lend a comforting ear, as Dennis Wilson did for me. Earlier in my life, after my freshman year in community college, I had flunked out and then contracted mono and hepatitis. I was wandering and had no idea what to do. Uncle Sam Greenstein was there for me. He picked me up, asked me what I was going to do, and facilitated a fresh start for me in a new location. There are people who care for you and are on your side.

Next, as hard as it may be, try to put the negative thoughts out of your own mind, and don't beat yourself up. We're often our own worst critics, and negative thoughts about ourselves are not only self-defeating, they are also self-fulfilling. Tell yourself, "I can get through this situation. I can do this." Instead of criticizing yourself, work on ways to build yourself up. Whatever bad stuff has happened, it has most likely happened at some time to someone else too; whatever mistakes have been made, it is certain that someone else made those same mistakes before. Instead of looking at blunders as something that must be avoided, learn from them, move on, and get better at what you do. Take ownership of your mistakes without internalizing the failure, and look at the adversities as obstacles you can overcome.

I like to empower my employees to make decisions, which is one reason I've had such success in retaining top people. My two general managers, Jake Sacks and Randy Habiger, have been with me for 17 and 27 years, respectively, and they'll tell you that my trust in them to manage the business is a big reason they've stayed with me all these years. Likewise, when times are tough and I've felt overwhelmed, I've learned to empower myself. I don't allow myself to play the victim, and I look to how quickly I can take control of whatever I can in the situation.

I always try to look at adversity as an opportunity for growth, not to pretend that difficulties aren't actually difficult, but to recognize that good things can come out of even the most dire of situations. When I was at my lowest, feeling that I was adrift at the age of 44, I admittedly had a negative attitude. But I determined then that I wanted to make it all work for my family and for my career, and I was tenacious in searching for the right opportunity so I could remain in the Kansas City area. Fortunately, I had resources and cash flow from my Decatur ventures, and that kept me on solid financial footing until I found the right situation. I kept the positives firmly in front of me and took solace from the fact that I was blessed with those opportunities. This gave me the impetus to get my circumstances in order so that everyone would benefit.

Above all, it's important to be a person of action, someone who analyzes their strengths and weaknesses and makes a plan to address life's challenges. Negative events and experiences can assist us only if we view them as a learning experience. In the moment, it may be hard to see what's good about them, but if we review what happened and what we can take from the experience, the results can become beneficial, and even empowering.

Life is a process. There are always ups and downs. We can't be so naïve to believe it's going to be a steady rise to the top, so we learn from the experience, take charge of our circumstances, and find our way through the tunnel and back out into the light.

Chapter 15
LEARN TO FIX YOUR OWN FLAT

Principle #15: Keep things in perspective

"When you play by the rules, defy mental demons, overcome every challenge, and enjoy a walk in the country at the same time — that's being alive."
Arnold Palmer

Life will throw you some curves. Adversity is a given in life, and at times it may seem overwhelming. As problem seems to pile upon problem, our troubles can consume our thoughts and can seem to grow so that they completely fill our field of vision, making it impossible to see anything else. At these times it's imperative to find ways to maintain a clear view of what's truly important in each situation, to keep things in perspective.

In 2006, my daughter Mandi separated from her husband. It was a tough situation, complicated by the fact that her husband worked in my dealership. One Sunday she came over to our house and told us it was over — a divorce was imminent. I hugged her and told her we would be there for her, and we would smother her with love as long as she needed and wanted it.

My Mom was in her mid-90s at the time, and mentally was still at the top of her game. She had always embraced her family, and never failed to open her home to relatives from near and far. She took pride in her children and was very close with her grandchildren and great-grandchildren. I knew I needed to call her and let her know about such an important and painful family event, but it took me a little while to muster up the courage to do so, as I could only imagine how disappointed and saddened she would be to hear the news. She's always put a high value on a strong marriage — when my dad died in 1994, he and Mom had been married 59 years. I didn't know what kind of reaction she would have to the news of divorce in the family.

Eventually I faced my fear and forced myself to pick up the phone and call her. When she answered, after some chit-chat I told her about Mandi and her husband getting a divorce. I said that as much as I hated to tell her, I still thought she should know. Then I waited…it seemed like hours of silence went by, but it was actually just a brief pause. I asked if she was okay. She said she was, and then inquired if I was okay. I told her I was just concerned about Mandi and her son and how this was all going to play out.

At that point she said something I will never forget: "The good news is that nobody died." It snapped me back to reality.

She then went through her philosophical assessment of the bonding of our family — how we were strong, would move on, and would collectively get through it. Even at her advanced age, Mom remained one of those people who knew how and what to say, as well as when to say it. In that short conversation of 10 or 15 minutes, she offered simple advice that reverberated with wisdom.

Mom had seen a lot in her long life. Not only had she outlived my father, she had also survived all her siblings as well as one of her grandsons (and my nephew), Brad Schifman, who died at the age of 28 in 1997. She had been raised on the stories and lived in the aftermath of the discrimination her forebears had suffered in their native countries, and she had friends who had escaped the Holocaust. She was more than just my mom. She was a wise and trusted advisor.

I had been around long enough to know that I needed to keep things in perspective, but Mom was still offering me a needed refresher on that life lesson. Despite the heartbreak of the situation, she reinforced that we still had a wonderful daughter with a healthy grandson. With some toil and tension, but more importantly with love and support, it ultimately turned out fine for Mandi and her son, Maddox, just as Mom reminded me it would. Mandi couldn't be a better mother as she lives her life based on what is best for him, and with her background in education she's putting him on the right path to success. He's now 15, and after having only daughters, it's nice to finally have another fella around — he's become my best buddy. He's a pretty good basketball player, too, and Paula and I enjoy attending his school and sporting events.

At a time when something had gone wrong, Mom reminded us that there was still much to be thankful for, that we should remain grateful, and that we would survive and thrive. This was typical of the calming presence she brought to our household when I was growing up. During my childhood, Dad was working most of the time, and she managed the house — and me — in a positive and caring manner. I know there were occasions when I disappointed her, but she never showed anger. Instead, she supported me and encouraged me. She gave me the freedom to make good decisions, but both she and Dad gave me a good foundation to know right from wrong. They made sure that I attended Hebrew school at the synagogue and learned the principles that have led me to a productive and meaningful life.

Mom showed benevolence to everyone and was always welcoming to friends and family alike — whether it be for one meal or several weeks of residency. When my aunt Ethel needed a place to stay for a while, she moved in with us. There was another family of shirttail relatives who had come to the area from another part of the country, and they lived with us until their new home was ready. She and my dad volunteered countless hours at the synagogue, and though they didn't have a lot of money they were generous with what they did have. They taught me that if you can spend your time helping people, then your value will go further than just writing checks, and that's been my mantra for my civic and charitable involvement.

Mom definitely had the right perspective on life. Using that perspective has served me well many occasions. There are three dictates I learned from her which I feel we all should follow, practices that help us keep our perspective in proper focus: do what's best to help our family and friends; serve our communities; and do what is right in the eyes of God. If we follow those three principles, we will treat everything else on our life's journey with the appropriate outlook and attitude, even when that includes setting aside our personal interests to appreciate the perspectives of others, then working through any obstacles or disagreements through collaboration.

Maintaining Mom's kind of perspective has helped me in many situations. There were times that the circumstances surrounding the Auto Plaza could have caused strain between me and the Van Tuyls as their business choices ran counter to my needs and desires, but in the end our relationship was strong, and our friendship endured. About the same time, the possibility of moving again was causing angst within my family, but when it was time to make a decision, the choice was easy — I would do what was best for Paula and my daughters.

It's also a perspective that allows me to appreciate how fortunate I've been. I try my best to put that into action by giving back to the communities in which I've lived and worked and by lending a hand to those people who've had to overcome poverty or a disability. That appreciation also helps mitigate times of stress and adversity like I faced in Illinois during the NCAA basketball investigation when my name was undeservedly dragged through the mud. I knew I had done nothing wrong and put my faith in a higher power.

Even with a good perspective on life and its tribulations, along the way it is natural to have doubts. Life does not provide certainty; it instead offers mystery, and as a result sometimes we should take a leap of faith. The Hebrew Bible shows us that all the fathers of our faith had doubts — Abraham, Moses, David, and plenty of others. Moses led the Israelites out of 400 years of slavery in Egypt, and at one point while wandering in the desert, many of them wanted to go back to Egypt, because they had doubts that Moses would lead them to the Promised Land of milk and honey. Even knowing the misery and pain of the enslavement they'd left behind, fear and worry over what lay ahead overwhelmed. Should we be surprised ourselves to come to moments of doubt? Having times of doubt that challenge our perspective is common and normal, even for people of faith. In fact, doubt can even be good — it can spur us to investigate and do research. It results in questions, which can be an opportunity for learning.

Keeping things in perspective is something I've tried to pass on to my associates. People get overly excited about circumstances or problems, so I try to calmly talk to them, let them air out their complaints, and then jointly we reach a solution. One of the expectations I have for my team is that if they're going to bring me a problem, they should also come prepared to suggest a solution, or maybe even two. Most of the time, though, a big part of the solution, certainly a big part of how they handle the situation, is in that calm talk, that shift toward clarity of vision and a resizing of the problem itself.

Right after Dale Backs died, I had to take over the general manager duties while I searched for a replacement. My first hire was the candidate I brought from outside the organization to run the body shop. I could sense early on that I had made a mistake. Shortly after the hire, the assistant who had been there and had remained came directly to see me. He told me he was doing the best he could to hold things together, but the new guy absolutely didn't know what he was doing. I was afraid my longtime employee was going to quit, but fortunately I talked him down and convinced him to hang in there with me. I told him to keep working hard, to make sure the technicians in his department did the same, and to give me some time. Knowing I understood where he was coming from and that I was working on the situation, he felt less alone. His perspective changed. He gave me the time I needed and soon after I let go of the manager and promoted that assistant to the position instead.

That same employee came to me a while later and told me that he was dating a woman who worked in the office. He said he understood that one of them would have to leave the organization, but he wanted me to know what was going on before I made a decision. I know they were both very nervous about the situation and how I would react. We addressed "Romantic Relationships" in our Employee Handbook, but since they were in different departments and neither supervised the other, it wasn't against our company policy. They were both valuable employees I was happy to retain, and they were relieved that they could let go of their borrowed trouble.

In both situations, a normally sensible and conscientious person was on the verge of making a rash decision. By listening to his worries and talking through the issue from a viewpoint other than his own tunnel vision, I retained a valuable member of the organization. I was glad that he came to me with his concerns — our environment of open communication in action — but I couldn't help but think of the stress he could have prevented for himself if he'd done so just a little sooner instead of hanging onto the worry.

My philosophy has always been to share the right perspective with my department heads so they'll understand there's no time or place for worry, faultfinding, self-criticism, self-defensiveness, complaining, or shifting blame. Problems are solved through a transparent exchange of ideas with no finger-pointing. After all, we must all be able to see that we are on the same team and working to make the organization as successful as possible.

Once, a general manager at one of my dealerships was having differences with a long-time department head, and the bad feelings between them were escalating. They really didn't get along and tried to stay away from each other, but eventually I had to intervene. I put things in perspective for them bluntly and told them that if they wanted to go outside and wrestle, then go for it. But if they wanted to behave like grownups instead, they needed to handle their disagreements so that it made sense for them and for the company. The general manager knew I supported him as the supervisor, and they came to a truce before the department head eventually retired.

Our two general managers at Crown Automotive, Jake Sacks and Randy Habiger, both started with our dealerships right out of college (Randy under the previous owner) and have made the steady climb up the corporate ladder to be my righthand guys today. When they were first appointed as department heads, with minimal experience in supervising personnel, there were times when every adverse situation seemed like a major crisis to them, and they felt like they had to come to me for the answers. As they matured into their positions and into a better perspective, I empowered them with more authority. I now have enough confidence in their ability to run the show in my absence that I'm able to travel with my family for long periods of time. I had the experience to share the proper outlook, and thus could serve as their mentor, as Cecil Van Tuyl and the management at Van Chevrolet did for me in the early 1970s. They've both turned out to be outstanding general managers with bright futures ahead.

There was one time, on a lighter note, that I had to help Randy keep his perspective. He's a big fan of the KU basketball team, and during the 2008 Final Four I had taken him along with Max Falkenstien to San Antonio for the games. He laughs about it now, but during the championship game between Kansas and Memphis Randy was a nervous wreck. With two minutes to play and the Jayhawks down by nine points, I looked over at him to see his head in his hands, convinced that defeat was imminent. I told him not to give up on the Jayhawks yet, as I felt sure they were about to mount a comeback. Anyone who is a diehard sports fan will know how deeply those feelings can run. I didn't want the potential defeat of our team to destroy Randy's enjoyment of the game or the experience of being there.

I wasn't as confident as I pretended to be about KU's chances, though, and my own stomach was churning in that moment, too. I was thinking about the long walk back to the hotel from the Alamodome after our team lost, in the midst of a bunch of reveling Memphis Tiger fans. But then Kansas made a furious rally, Memphis missed some free throws, and with 2.1 seconds remaining Mario Chalmers hit a three-pointer to tie the game at 63. In overtime, we saw Kansas outscore the Tigers 12-5 in the extra period to win their first national title in 20 years. Our walk back to the hotel wasn't so bad after all, and we were among the Kansas fans who did the reveling. I was even able to muster a little sympathy for all those Memphis fans. Sort of.

Perspective throughout the organization is enhanced by open and transparent communication. Employees want and need to know what is happening, especially in uncertain times. They want consistent and open feedback. An email blast may be the most efficient way to get out a broad message, but the most effective communication is a direct conversation, by phone or in person, with a preference for the latter. That is another reason I like to walk around my stores on a regular basis. If the staff knows I'm engaged and aware of what's happening in the company and with them personally, they are more likely to have a positive and collaborative attitude. Sometimes called "management by wandering around," it provides an unstructured method for encouraging honest feedback.

It is deep-rooted in true leaders to maintain their perspective. They are in their positions because they are problem solvers who recognize and accept different viewpoints and have access to more information. The more information they have, the more effective they are in their role as the captain of the team. They can embrace setbacks as challenges and have the confidence to work jointly with others to seek the optimal solution. They take the time to evaluate the alternatives and arrive at a course of action they think is best. If a decision is unsuccessful, the effective leader asks what was done wrong and what can be done to prevent the situation from reoccurring. If it is successful, they take note of why it was so that the process can be repeated in the future.

Perspective is paramount in dealing with customers as well. In handling a situation with a customer who is upset, I counsel our staff to use a calming presence rather than escalating the situation. I've had irate customers almost threaten me (like the time that guy wanted to drive his car up my butt) but responding in a like manner does nothing to solve the problem. It's all about perspective — try to think as the customer is thinking. Tell them you understand the situation in a cool and reserved manner, which goes a long way in helping all the parties involved get on the same page. Do everything within reason to make it right, and don't be concerned if you sacrifice a few hundred dollars to fix the problem. Every customer represents a particular dollar amount in their lifetime as a potential buyer, and it's a lot of money. If you're going to alienate them over a small amount, it may actually cost tens of thousands of dollars of revenue in the end. That's a philosophy preached throughout my entire organization and is a big reason our dealership has one of the highest rates of repeat customers in our region.

Furthermore, human nature dictates that once someone has a bad experience somewhere, they are likely to aggressively spread the word, and that is even more common today with ease of access to the internet and the multitude of social media possibilities — also bad for business. Even if they never say anything negative, it's far better to have the customer come to you with a complaint rather than let them go somewhere else. So make them happy. When handled well, upset customers can turn into your greatest allies. Many times, a relationship is enhanced after a successful resolution of a problem, so it's best to address the problem rather than run from it. Customers leave feeling that they've received high quality special treatment because the company representative went out of their way to assist. They become return customers because they know they will be treated well. This strategy is an effective way to grow your business and increase long-term customer loyalty.

Maintaining perspective has helped me weather the storm many times in my career as a business owner. When something in the outside world has the potential to adversely affect our business, I can't take time to fret about what I can't control. Since I took over management of my first dealership in 1979, there has been a steady stream of political crises, gas shortages, recessions, corporate bankruptcies, automotive industry recalls and scandals, a pandemic, and more besides — all of which have affected my dealerships. Obviously, I didn't cause any of these situations, but my team and I sure felt the impact. If I had been inclined to hit the panic button, there's a chance my business wouldn't have survived. We adjusted, made modifications to our practices and budgets, and in almost every case came out stronger than we had been before these events. Our department heads didn't look around at each other or at me with fear in their eyes and ask, "What the heck are you going to do about this?" They closed ranks with me, and we looked at these as group problems whose solutions needed each person's attention and cooperation. With this group-based viewpoint, we persevered.

Even the COVID-19 pandemic has been manageable. It has presented some unique trials, though, since the country had not experienced anything like it for more than a century, and we have been in unfamiliar territory. We're working our way through it (and hoping we're in the final stage). But again, we kept our cool through the initial shock and the early lockdowns, adjusted our sales model along with our budgets, and soon after people were back buying cars. Support from the government through the Payroll Protection Program (PPP) loans was also a big help financially. The biggest challenge going forward has been getting new product from the manufacturers, but overall we've continued to have a solid financial performance and did not have to lay off staff. I feel very fortunate in that regard.

• • • •

It's all well and good to say, "Maintain a healthy perspective," but a lot harder to do in practice. So here are a few practical suggestions that have helped me over the years. As with most things, these are good habits to follow in the good times. In the difficult times, when our perspective is most likely to get out of whack, it's the habitual nature of our actions that can protect us from going off the rails.

Focus on what you can control. If you allow what you can't control to affect your disposition and add to your frustration, you're guaranteed to be an ineffective leader. There are always circumstances beyond your control that will try to consume your attention. But it's how you respond to what you can control that's most important. This is what the people around you will remember. It's also the only way to keep moving forward in a crisis.

Listen to those around you. Likewise, avoid simply directing people. In sales we are taught to let the prospective customer do more of the talking. As managers we should do the same. Rather than giving orders to employees, let them talk, and be willing to learn from them, as they are the ones with the boots on the ground. The more information and understanding you have, the better decisions you'll make when it's time for you to do so.

Set long-term goals. Even as you have these goals, know from the start that they will need to be reviewed and adjusted according to changing circumstances. There are many outside factors that make it difficult to project 10 years, or even three, down the road. But as I've stated before, it's important to have an idea of what to shoot for, even in generalities. Breaking those goals down into one-year, three-month, and 30-day goals will help you keep the proper perspective on inevitable disruptions so that they won't throw you overboard.

Stay connected. Whether you're an introvert or an extrovert, you need a community. It's true that community looks different for different people, but you were not built to go through life only on your own steam and brainpower. Other people hold us up and give us a chance to learn from others' experiences as well as our own.

Keep yourself healthy. Work on your fitness and eating habits to reduce stress and give you one less thing (your own physical well-being) to worry about. Unexpected health problems that we can't plan for do occur and we must all face them as they come, but as I focus on what I can control, my own general fitness is one of those things. I exercise regularly to maintain my health, and I also stick to a healthy diet that usually has me ordering salads instead of fried or greasy foods. I may get some grief from my friends who love the steaks and barbecue, but I sure feel good for a guy in his 70s.

Take time to reflect on what has occurred each day. This includes what went right, what went wrong, how you addressed each circumstance, and what you can do better next time. You'll find yourself more prepared to face problems, and you may also realize the problems may not have been as bad as they seemed when they originally surfaced.

Find hobbies that you really enjoy. More than that, make a regular point of scheduling times to participate in them. This helps you avoid tunnel vision. Hobbies take your focus off other issues and gives you something to look forward to on your daily schedule. I try to have regular golf outings on my calendar and to spend as much time as I can with my grandson.

I include these practices in my own life and encourage my employees to do the same. When we can all achieve a measure of perspective that balances the stressful and the restful, work and personal, physical and mental, then together the business does better and, more importantly, we're better and happier people.

• • • •

My mom always said that everything works out for the best in the end, and that's the philosophy I've used in addressing the challenging managerial situations. She was a woman of great faith, and always a believer in positive fate. I've inherited that belief, and I've tried to pass it on to my family and employees. There are bumps along the way and things may not always be going right, but stay with the task, keep your perspective positive, and, more often than not, the situation will work in your favor. Maintaining a capacity for gratitude certainly helps. More than that, it improves your quality of life. I'm thankful for where I am and what I have, tangible and intangible, and I'm willing to share whatever is needed. The sense of feeling grateful enhances my general outlook.

I have always been fortunate to have family and friends who provide balance and perspective in my life. I hung around with kids who were from good, solid families. My parents were born in the United States but came from families who had experienced religious discrimination in their homelands. We knew other families in which the parents had escaped Germany and Eastern Europe immediately prior to or during the Holocaust. With backgrounds such as those, you learn some lessons about perspective early on.

My parents' generation knew that any tragedy or genuine cataclysm could happen at any time, so they told us to do the right thing and we'd eventually be rewarded. We were taught to practice our faith and to be compassionate, to look out for our friends, neighbors, and the community beyond. My parents and those of my peers stressed being good citizens and staying out of trouble. They didn't press us to be overachievers. Just do your best and enjoy life, they told us, for you never know when it can drastically change. Be ready for and open to new opportunities.

In that same vein, we were taught to eliminate negativity, and for the most part the friends and family I grew up around were very positive people who were always willing to lend a helping hand. Complaining about petty things wasn't just unacceptable, it was never even considered. These lessons stuck with me. In business or in life, we tend to get upset when we lose something or we make a mistake, and in few cases are the results catastrophic. Material items can be replaced, and mistakes can be corrected.

On a more global scale, I feel that the proper perspective could help bridge a lot of the differences we have in our country and our world today. Again, I think back on the roots of my faith and my religious heritage as an example. The persecution of those of the Jewish faith throughout history is well-documented. My ancestors and the parents of some of my childhood friends witnessed far more horrific events than we have ever seen in the United States. Knowing these stories and appreciating how lucky I am to live in a land of opportunity gives me an optimistic perspective on the world today. I hear people stressing about the divides in our country, and want to say, "let's take a deep breath and calm down." I myself have lived through the civil rights movement, the Vietnam War, 9/11, the Great Recession, and COVID-19. Our current issues are fixable.

Why not enjoy and appreciate what we have? The daily stuff that drives you crazy — don't worry about it. Process those little irritants and press on. Because most of the time, Mom will still be right — nobody died.

THE MIRACLE WITH MIKE

There **was** another chance meeting I had with a sports legend that I like to share with people. Everybody in America knows about the 1980 Olympic Hockey Team and the "Miracle on Ice" victory over the heavily favored Soviet Union. Those Winter Olympic Games took place in Lake Placid, New York, and if you're over 50, you probably remember where you were when you heard the final score. If you're younger than that you've likely read one of the many books written about that team or watched the movie Miracle based on their evolution and ultimate triumph in winning the gold medal. Next to Jackie Robinson's major league debut in 1947, the Miracle on Ice was considered by many historians to be the most significant sports event of the 20th century.

I have two distinct remembrances of that game. The first is of the legendary sportscaster Al Michaels describing the final seconds with his famous call of "Do you believe in miracles? YES!" The other is the emotion shown by team captain Mike Eruzione after he scored what proved to be the winning goal midway through the third period.

Eruzione played his college hockey at Boston University, the same school my younger daughter, Ali, would later attend. During my time in business in the Kansas City area, I became acquainted with a local entrepreneur and County Commissioner named Dave Lindstrom, who had played eight seasons as a defensive end for the Kansas City Chiefs and was a football player at Boston University around the same time that Eruzione played hockey there.

We've made a lot of trips to Boston over the years since Ali was in school there, and she has made her home in the Boston area ever since. Mike Eruzione still resides in that region, and in addition to his public speaking gigs he has worked for the school — first as an assistant coach and currently as its Director of Special Outreach. Dave wanted to connect the two of us on one of our family trips, so he gave me Mike's phone number, and most every time I went to Boston I'd call him to try to get together. We'd talk, and actually became friends over the phone, but our schedules never worked out so that we could meet in person.

I was at a regional Toyota dealer's meeting in Florida in the mid-2000s, as the Kansas City Toyota dealers like to do these meetings offsite at a resort. We would always have a guest speaker at the end of a day-long seminar, and the organizers would make it a surprise person of renown. Among them have been such dignitaries as George W. Bush and Condoleezza Rice.

Since I'm on the National Dealers Council I was sitting up front, when they announced, "Our guest speaker for today is ..." a clip of the Miracle on Ice began to play on the big screen, "... Mike Eruzione!" My reaction was, "Damn — I feel like I've known the guy for years but now I'm finally going to get to meet him." While he was talking all I could think about was wanting him to hurry up so that I could introduce myself. I'm not sure I listened to a word he said.

When he finished, I rushed to where he was and introduced myself. We talked like old buddies. Everyone else was trying to push to the front to get his autograph, and I just stood there and visited with him. The others looked at me as if to say, "move along," but I didn't care. It was my chance to talk to an American sports icon, and I wasn't going to cut it short for anybody.

I won't call it a "miracle" that we finally connected in person, but it was sure serendipitous. It would be a great understatement to say it was a thrill for me to finally meet the man who was the face of the legendary 1980 U.S. Olympic Hockey Team. In a challenging period of American history, when the country was in an economic malaise and despondent about the ongoing Iran hostage crisis, a remarkable collection of young men from different parts of the country brought Americans together to witness one of the greatest upsets in sports history. He and that whole team represented something hopeful and optimistic at a time when those were hard feelings to find. It kind of feels like we could use another one of those moments.

It's time to be hopeful and optimistic again. Do you believe in miracles?

Chapter 16
YOU'RE BEHIND THE WHEEL

Principle #16: Control Your Own Destiny

"God has given me the ability. The rest
is up to me. Believe, believe, believe."
Billy Mills

Fans of the Kansas City Chiefs will recognize the name of Kendall Gammon, who forged a 15-year career as a long snapper in the NFL — seven of those seasons with the Chiefs. While playing a variety of positions for Pittsburg State's 1991 Division II national championship team, Kendall started experimenting with long snapping duties before his sophomore season. After a poor snap in his initial spring scrimmage, he decided he never wanted to be embarrassed on the field again, and he devoted himself to mastering the skills of the position. In his junior year, an NFL scout named Vinny Cerrato told Kendall that he was one of the top long snappers in the nation, in any division. Kendall suddenly realized that if he continued to practice, he might be able to make a living playing football.

Kendall was drafted by the Pittsburgh Steelers in the 11th round of the 1992 NFL draft. He played four seasons for the Steelers, even appearing in Super Bowl XXX, and followed that with four years in New Orleans before signing with the Chiefs in 2000. He was named to the Pro Bowl after the 2004 season — the first pure long snapper to be selected for that all-star game. During one remarkable streak in his career, he played in 218 consecutive games.

Kendall worked at his craft as hard as anyone who's ever played the game. In fact, he revolutionized his position. Long snapping wasn't even considered a specialty in the NFL until he made it one, and now every team has a player on its roster whose only job is to be the long snapper — much like there are designated specialists to be the placekicker and the punter.

An offensive lineman and tight end in college, Kendall spent hours perfecting this skill once he knew that it could be his ticket to the NFL. He would snap the ball to whoever would catch it in the Pitt State athletic facility, and if no one was around he'd snap it against the wall. He made it a science. In his rookie year with the Steelers, veteran placekicker Gary Anderson came up to him at training camp and asked him if he could snap the ball so that the laces would always face out for the holder and kicker. Kendall said he'd give it a try, and through his training regimen he determined it took exactly three-and-a-half rotations for the ball to be in that optimal "laces-out" position. Which he achieved.

How important was his specialty to his team? In 2005, he missed a game because of injury, and a late field goal attempt was missed by the Chiefs after a low snap. It not only cost the Chiefs a chance at a win, but they ultimately missed the playoffs by one game. The team that beat them out for the last playoff spot was the Pittsburgh Steelers — who went on to win the Super Bowl that year.

Kendall is a prime example of someone who made the choice to control his destiny. He was determined to find success in the NFL, even as a player from a smaller Division II school. Realistically understanding that his chances to be a regular as an offensive lineman were limited, he focused on something he could control — his ability to become the best at his craft, albeit an initially unexpected craft.

After his retirement from pro football, Kendall has worked as a motivational speaker, authored two books, and, from 2016 to 2019, was also the color analyst on the Chiefs Radio Network. He is currently a special assistant in external relations to the president at Pitt State. His motto for his website is, appropriately enough, "Laces Out," and he has a new podcast called *The Extra Point* in which he and his guests explore how to be successful and make a difference in the world.

Kendall and I met at a charity golf tournament when he was still playing with the Chiefs, and through our common affiliation with Pitt State we struck up an easy conversation. His agent later contacted me about supplying a car for him to drive, but I was hesitant, as I'd had a bad experience with a previous Chiefs player who returned a courtesy vehicle in rather less than pristine condition. But Kendall convinced me that wouldn't happen with him, and I agreed.

Since then, we've become close friends, and I have great admiration for everything he's accomplished. Through dedication and practice he became the very best in his field, carving a new path that no one before him had considered, and he continues to inspire me with his life now. When our family decided to make a more impactful contribution to Pittsburg State, he was the one who helped guide us to the area where we could make the most difference — the new HVAC system and video board at the John Lance Arena. It may not seem very sexy, but neither is sweating through a sporting event without being able to watch a clear replay, and I know it's been appreciated and put to good use.

I've been fortunate to find inspiration in both old friends and new. I was recently able to reconnect with an old childhood buddy named Harry Friedman who forged a unique path for himself as well. Harry grew up in Omaha, and he and I were both active members of the Synagogue Youth Organization (SYO) in our respective cities. I met him at one of our conventions when we were kids, and even though we lived in different states we were friends. He also had cousins who lived down the street from me in Kansas City, and we all spent some time together attending Camp Moshava, a Jewish youth camp in central Wisconsin.

A great guy from a great family, Harry always had a smile on his face. He was always fascinated by television and the people who made a living from it, and he created a sort of internship for himself at the local television stations, long before such things existed, doing and learning whatever they'd allow. Then in 1971, at the age of 24, Harry decided it was time to control his destiny, and he moved to Los Angeles without a job or any contacts. He gave himself six months to land a gig in show business, and with just 24 hours left before his deadline he was hired as a part-time question writer on the old *Hollywood Squares* game show. He stayed there and eventually became a writer and producer, then proceeded to become a producer for such shows as *Wheel of Fortune* and *Jeopardy*. His 14 Emmys are the most ever won by the producer of a game show, and among his many other honors he was given a star on the Hollywood Walk of Fame in 2019. Not bad for a kid from Nebraska with an unlikely dream.

It's not just the big, well-known accomplishments that inspire me, though. I've become a big supporter of organizations that help people with disabilities, and in my reading and research of individuals who've triumphed over a physical limitation I've come across two men who have been particularly moving, and who epitomize the control of one's destiny perhaps better than anyone else, since they both had more obstacles to overcome.

The first is Ralph Braun, the founder of BraunAbility, a manufacturer of vans, ramps, and lifts for wheelchairs based in Indiana. Ralph became known as the "Father of the Mobility Movement" after creating one of the earliest wheelchair accessible vehicles in the 1960s, and then introducing the first wheelchair accessible minivan in the early 1990s. At the age of six, he was diagnosed with muscular dystrophy, and his parents were told he would never be independent. By the age of 14 he was in a wheelchair, but he set his mind to engineering motorized devices that could help him get around — first a wagon and later a scooter, both by the age of 20. Within a few years he had founded the company that would later become BraunAbility, driven by his desire to live independently and provide other people with physical disabilities the chance to participate fully in life. Ralph Braun raised five children, and with one of his sons owned a NASCAR racing team, before he passed away in 2013 at the age of 72. His employees and friends remember him as a man who never made excuses. And he motivated others to live the same way every day.

The second, Craig MacFarlane grew up in a small town in Ontario, Canada, where he lost his sight in a tragic accident at the age of two. Because there were limited support services near their family farm, Craig's parents raised him with no special treatment. As his mother said, "We didn't know how to raise a blind kid, so we just raised a kid."

He was required by law to attend a school for the blind more than 500 miles from his home, but Craig wanted to return to the sighted world and be with his family and friends. He found his opportunity through wrestling, in which he won against sighted competition. Expanding his interests to other sports, he proved he could thrive and was eventually allowed to attend high school back in his hometown.

Craig became an outstanding track and field athlete, winning numerous gold medals at blind national championships, and later took up skiing — both on the snow and the water. In 1983 he won the U.S. Blind National Downhill Snow Skiing Championship with a final run in which his speed exceeded 50 miles per hour. That same year he won the U.S. Blind Water-Skiing Championship and was offered a contract to join the famous Cypress Gardens Water Ski Jumping Show Team, thus becoming the first totally blind professional athlete. He's even broken 100 playing golf and was part of the torch relay for the 1984 Los Angeles Olympics, where he ran with his friend and hockey legend Gordie Howe. Now a longtime author and motivational speaker, he was even asked by Ronald Reagan to speak at the 1984 Republican National Convention.

All these people seized the day and controlled their destiny. Even though their circumstances were markedly different, each had a dream, but more importantly a commitment, to succeed. Kendall Gammon was determined to play in the NFL and knew the only way he could get there was to develop a special skill. Harry Friedman was a normal kid growing up in the Midwest, but he took a chance and moved to the epicenter of an industry that intrigued him despite having no contacts. Ralph Braun was told he would never be able to live independently, and his response was to revolutionize mobility for individuals using a wheelchair, raise a family, and become a NASCAR team owner. And Craig MacFarlane, who just wanted to live and go to school near his hometown, used excellence in sports simply as a way to get home and then as a way to thrive in a sighted world that never seemed quite able to fathom his determination.

• • • •

My own story of controlling my destiny is not so dramatic, but it was a determination I had to make early in my career. I knew that if I didn't, then other people or circumstances would, and that was not going to be acceptable. When an opportunity presented itself, even one as simple as being the first salesperson to greet a customer on the showroom floor, I had to be ready to grab it, because no one was going to do it for me. I started offering to do any task needed by the dealership, to come in early and stay late, and to learn what everyone in every department was doing. I wanted to be that shining star so I would get chosen when it was time for a promotion or special assignment.

And it's a business where a professional appearance is important, so I took extra care with mine. We're selling to the public, and thus need to eliminate any distractions in the sales interaction. I always joked that if you have a piece of food in your teeth, the person you're addressing is going to be more focused on that food than what you're saying. The same is true of clothes. Dressing your best means perception, because if you look sharp it gives customers the impression that you know what you're doing. If your clothes are not appropriate, of substandard material, or there are some loose threads, then that's the lasting impression you'll leave, instead of any wisdom you may have imparted.

That's why I still wear a suit and tie to work every day. Even after all these years, I still want to look my best and help further establish our brand. When I was in Decatur a lot of people shopped at the same men's store, and when I'd go into business meetings I'd notice that there were as many as three or four other people who had on the same suit I did. I decided then that at some point in my life, when I could afford it, I'd have custom suits so I wouldn't just look like everyone else. It's a subtle way to be in control of whatever situation I find myself in, so that when I meet people, they will remember me in a positive light. It also makes me feel better and more confident in myself. I think it's probably working, because even Bill Self once autographed a basketball for me with an inscription that described me as "the best-dressed guy in the room." But that's just me. Find your own way to stand out in the crowd and be the one they remember. Visuals help — pick the one that works for you.

Early in my career I tried to observe sales techniques and soak up as much knowledge as possible from those with experience as another way to shape my trajectory. I learned how important it was to control the sales process, thanks in part to the mentorship of Jerry Dahmer, our general manager at Van Chevrolet. He stressed patience in dealing with a prospective buyer, teaching us that you should wait until your customer is ready to make a decision rather than rush them into it. To no one's surprise, Jerry had a lot of success with his own dealerships before he sold them in 2003 — another guy who controlled his own destiny.

And of course I learned a lot from Cecil Van Tuyl about being a manager and running an operation smoothly. I knew that whenever I took over a dealership I needed to be intimately involved with every phase of the operation. When he first made me a business partner in charge of the stores in Decatur, I was all of 32 years old and moving to an unfamiliar market. I thought I was pretty good, but I found out right away the dealership was underperforming, and I would have to make some changes — to the dealership and to my own plan for management.

Fortunately, I had already learned that an important element of controlling my own destiny was understanding that I couldn't really do it on my own. I needed to have good people around me who would be looking for ways to be mutually successful, and I had to know who had my back. Fortunately, in Decatur I was lucky to inherit a new car manager, Pat Dawson, and a used car manager, Bob Brilley, who had both been at the dealership for years, knew the market well, and were good at their jobs. They were both Catholic, and in a small city with five Catholic churches and only one synagogue, they were a big help in introducing me to a significant portion of the local community. Those two were part of my own inner sanctum, and my right-hand guys in running the operation.

We had to sift through a lot of personnel — a surprising amount based on the longevity of the dealership. I gave people a chance to succeed, but as soon as I realized it wasn't going to work out it was best to shake hands and part company. Since Pat and Bob knew a lot of folks in the area, they could point me in the direction to get the best new people on board, and eventually we had the right staff in place.

I operated in total synchrony with them, which gave us all the opportunity to do our best work and forge our paths forward. They knew me so well that they could tell what I needed and when I needed it with very little effort. One time this young man who had bought a car from us came into the dealership to speak to me. He had decided he couldn't afford the car and wanted us to buy it back. We sat together in my office as I listened to him talk, but I had to tell him that though I could sympathize with his request, I couldn't take the car back. He had a loan on it with GMAC and he would have to work through them. I told him I'd like to help him, but it had to be between him and GMAC, and I gave him their number.

He began to insist, in louder and more forceful tones, and I began to get nervous. This went on for a while, and Pat could see us through the window in my office and knew something wasn't right. It took only an inquiring look from him and a nod from me and he came in my office to ask about the situation. Pat heard the guy's complaint, together he and I made it clear that we couldn't buy the car back, and then Pat escorted him outside. Where my voice alone wasn't enough to be convincing or calming, as a team we managed the moment. Pat definitely had my back.

As I said, there were a lot of things — and attitudes — to fix in those early days in Decatur, but Bob and Pat helped keep us steady through the transition. Business as usual wasn't going to help us move forward or help anyone be successful in the long-term, wouldn't help anyone control their destiny, but the changes often made the short-term seem worse to those who had benefitted from business as usual. If I'd been concerned with only the immediate, I wouldn't have been able to make the decisions that corrected financial inequities and reduced or changed staff. These were hard decisions, but they're also the ones that kept us a viable business and then turned us into a thriving one.

I had to make even bigger changes when I completed the purchase of the Lawrence stores, which had been plagued by substandard management and business practices and suffered from a poor reputation in the community. I had no preconceived notion that I was going to step in, put my feet up on the desk, and just be an absentee owner. It took me some time to get the right staff in place. Until I had the operation up and running and could attract the best people, I had to be prepared to do any job.

I brought Dale over from Decatur as soon as I could, and he was a godsend. Since then, I've been fortunate to have Randy Habiger to run the Toyota shop, and later Jake Sacks to supervise Volkswagen. I'm at a good point now where I can trust them and their department heads to do the job. And with the business and our relationships as solid as they are, Randy, Jake, and others are in a position where they can make strong choices about their own destinies.

• • • •

When asked for advice on how to control one's destiny, I always advise that the first step is to have some self-awareness — understanding where you are, where you'd like to be, and then to evaluate what is realistically attainable versus what is truly unrealistic. For example, if someone loves classical music but has a tin ear, they may practice their singing for hours upon hours, but they can't expect to become the lead soloist at the Metropolitan Opera. However, they may turn their attention toward production or staging and forge a career in the entertainment industry. Evaluate your skills, talents, and desires honestly, without varnish but also without self-deprecation, to determine your starting point, and make your life's plan from there.

Then take charge of that over which you have control and forget about the rest. What you can command more than anything else is your own state of mind. Have a goal, have a purpose, and block out any self-doubts. For instance, I've always told my managers that their jobs are to run the day-to-day operations of the dealerships and leave the outside distractions up to me. I'll take care of working with the manufacturers and lobbying for help with the politicians. Come to work every day, expect to be successful, make your plan, and control what you can control.

And since you can't control the past, don't dwell on it. If you've failed at something but still believe you can be successful, then let go of the past failure — stop letting it hurt you in the present. Take whatever lessons there were in it, allow the experience to help you grow into a better version of yourself, and keep facing forward.

Evaluate your relationships and gravitate to those people who support and believe in you. Avoid the naysayers who will just bring you down. It will be impossible to avoid all doubts — from those looking on, from friends and family, even from yourself — especially if you're trying something new or unexpected. But the voices that ring the loudest, the voices you listen to most, should be the ones that build you up.

We also need to be able to recognize opportunities when they come along and embrace them. They should be challenging, pushing us to new levels of achievement, but they must also be consistent with our value system. If they look too good to be true then they likely are, and we must be willing to pass on opportunities if there is even a chance that our integrity or standards would be compromised. New opportunities should generate excitement and energy and get our juices flowing and the wheels in our mind turning. We need to be cautious about letting that excitement cloud our ability to clearly evaluate and pull us into pie-in-the-sky ventures that are simply drains on time and generate nothing of value.

In a nutshell, the path to success is up to our individual choice. Nobody is going to take the initiative for us, but that doesn't mean that we can't rely on others for assistance. It really comes down to taking personal responsibility for the path we pursue. Some people manage to luck into opportunities, but more often we need to generate our own. If we wait for someone to create them for us, we'll likely be sitting around a long time, and eventually it will be too late. Missteps and goals that weren't quite reached are easier to live with than the regret of never trying.

We're blessed to live in a society where we get to control our own destiny, as there are millions of people around the world who live in situations where simple survival is the only goal. How we each choose to take advantage of the blessing of living here and now is up to us.

Chapter 17
EXPECT THE BEST

Principle #17: Believe in
yourself or nobody else will

*"The quality of a person's life is in direct
proportion to their commitment to excellence,
regardless of their chosen field of endeavor."*
Vince Lombardi

When I came back from Kansas City and was sitting
in the back of the room in my first meeting at the
Auto Plaza, ready to face 82 salespeople as the United States
military was entering Kuwait, I thought I might still have time
to bail on this venture and move back to Decatur, since my
family hadn't moved yet. My first inclination was to say, "Why
me?" But the more I thought about it, the more my frame
of mind changed. On that morning during that introductory
meeting, I took a negative feeling and turned it into a positive.
"Why not me?" I began asking myself. After all, if not me,
then who else? With that simple shift, I began to transform

a sort of victim mentality into an attitude of resiliency and confidence.

Self-confidence in your ability to do the job is a hallmark of effective leadership. Self-confidence isn't necessarily intuitive; it is often an acquired trait that is developed and enhanced through solid practices. Early in my career, I was fortunate to have mentors who would sit me down and encourage me to develop good work habits. They would be blunt, inquiring about what I was doing on a daily basis. "Are you really working," they would ask, "or are you just slacking off?" They may have used rather stronger terms, but you get the picture.

There's a lot of "slacking off" that I've seen happen over the years. A salesperson might sell a few cars and start to feel full of themselves (and get to acting "rich and good-lookin'"). They'd think they'd arrived, but then all of a sudden, the drought would hit, they'd realize they weren't such a hotshot, and their confidence would dissipate. When that happened to me, I learned to ride it out. I didn't blame myself, avoided the "woe is me" attitude, and pressed on until things turned around. I truly believed — and was encouraged to believe by those I trusted — that I had the right habits to succeed over time.

I also had the help of great support — namely my wife. If I was a little under the weather, or had a bad day at work, she wouldn't sit around at home and hold my hand and baby me. She was very good at pushing me forward and supporting me in a positive manner. Having a support staff — or, in my case, a support person — who knows you and your personality is an invaluable part of not getting down on yourself. They're the ones who will be able to see when you need encouragement, when you need space, and when you need some tough love.

Having people with that kind of outlook supporting you will

also help you avoid distractions that could undermine the good work habits you're trying to develop. After I returned home from college and started my job, my fraternity brothers and old high school buddies would call me to go to Kansas City Royals games or hang out with them on Saturday afternoons to shoot baskets or play golf. I declined, albeit with some reluctance, because I knew I had to make the best of my job. Even when I was unsure of committing to auto sales as a career, I knew that I had to have a strong work ethic — just as my dad and my early mentors did. I could sleep in, call in sick if I had a few sniffles, and just show up the required number of hours. Or I could be the guy who came in early, stayed late, and worked every Saturday. I chose to be the latter. I believed in myself, and I believed in the possibilities, so I worked to bring them into existence.

I think Dad would be proud of me.

I also have a couple of friends who come to mind when I'm looking for an encouraging reminder in the power of self-belief, people I know and admire who believed in themselves and went on to success. One is Steve Brace, the fraternity brother from Pittsburg State who introduced me to Paula. Even then, Steve always had an affinity for snow skiing. In the late 1960s, his mom started a small boutique shop that sold high-end clothing for tennis and skiing, and then in the winter it would also sell basic ski equipment. When Steve graduated from college in 1972, he went to work with her and expanded to the rental of ski equipment, and he later opened a travel side to set up ski trips and sell lift tickets. That's still the crux of the business, but today they also sell equipment and clothing for skiing, snowboarding, wakeboarding, water skiing, and skateboarding. Against most logic and expectations, Steve believed in himself and his ability to make a ski shop thrive in the middle of the plains of the Midwest, while also competing against big box stores. He's now the president of Sitzmark Sports and has built a successful niche business rooted in a mountain sport — in Overland Park, Kansas.

Another friend who inspires me is Brian Hanni. Brian has been the play-by-play voice of the University of Kansas football, baseball, and men's basketball for the last six years, but we first got to know each other years earlier when he was the sports director at a local radio station and I was a sponsor of his show. After graduating from KU in 2002, he worked locally for 10 years broadcasting women's basketball and baseball for the Jayhawks, but his dream was to eventually become the voice for the KU's highest profile sports. He knew he needed to bolster his résumé before that could happen, though. On the advice of Coach Bill Self, he moved to Lubbock, Texas, to become the radio announcer for the Texas Tech Red Raiders. When the legendary Bob Davis retired as KU's play-by-play guy, Brian was ready — he now had the experience and the know-how he needed, and he got the job.

I have a lot of respect for both Steve and Brian for defying the odds and having the belief that they could make their businesses and careers work. Sure, dues were paid, but common among all of us was that we'd do whatever we had to do to get the job done and eliminate the outside distractions and negativity. We all believed we could reach our goals and knew when to go with our gut and when to take some timely advice from those we trusted.

Some people never figure out how to believe in themselves or, even sadder to me, some start out with a high level of self-confidence but give up at the first sign of failure. So how do we know that we can believe in ourselves and sustain that belief? Believing in our ability to achieve sometimes takes a leap of faith and a determination to endure in the face of setbacks. We need to draw on our life experiences when we are faced with difficult decisions and choices. Remembering and focusing on what we've already achieved gives us the foundation to believe in ourselves. We may need to start with small things as we build that foundation but, as with any foundation, brick by brick it becomes larger and stronger and more capable of holding more weight.

One way to enhance belief in yourself is to identify your weaknesses and, instead of shying away from them or getting down about them, find ways to address them. Even if they never transform into strengths, that work can prevent them from being limitations. This will increase your confidence and your belief that the sky is the limit in your quest for achievement. Also think about those past experiences to judge how far you've come. As a simple example, if you've set a goal to break 80 in golf and you still have done no better than a 90, remember when you couldn't break 100, and use that to measure your improvement and remind yourself that you're on the right track and still have cause to be confident in yourself.

Our beliefs go a long way in determining outcomes. If we don't have a firm belief in ourselves or in an idea or a task, we will hesitate to take action. I firmly maintain that everyone has some ability that will enable them to do great things, but if the drive or confidence is not there it likely will never happen. Great things look different in the lives of different people, but without the self-assurance, they will all go undone and the world will be less rich for it.

Belief in yourself is only the beginning, however. Your beliefs don't make you a better person; your behaviors do. And that's the most difficult part, particularly for someone who is in charge of other people or a situation. That means setting examples commensurate with being a leader and acting in a such a way that your employees and associates know you're not afraid of the responsibility of being in charge. It means walking upright with a sense of purpose.

Part of walking upright is figuring out how to balance that confidence and determination to succeed with a set of essential and shaping values. And the ideal may not always match the reality. Finding that balance, however, will help you know when to stand firm and when to shift out of necessity or practicality. For instance, one of my beliefs is to try and make everybody happy, but the reality is that my behavior can't always mirror that. Knowing when it's time to step up and say, "You're wrong," either to an employee or a customer, is essential and comes with experience and confidence. Your values may need to be given room to breathe with the situation, but you can never cross that line and break them, or you lose credibility in the long run. In our industry, or for that matter in any business that relies on retail sales, there are going to be ups and downs based on the environment and the economy. I may have to adjust, but I will never cross that line between right and wrong.

A lot of my motivation these days comes from watching people who work for me gain their own confidence and succeed. I have a salesman who was formerly a social worker for the state of Kansas before he came to work for us. He's frequently been the top salesperson at our dealership, and with that success has developed a lot of confidence in his ability. He doesn't want to be a manager; he just wants to keep selling 20 to 25 cars a month, and he makes pretty good money doing just that. He is continuing to hone his craft and reach the goal that he sets for himself.

We have another young salesman on the used car side who is very self-confident and does a great job in taking care of the customer. I have no hesitation about recommending friends and family to him because I know they'll be in good hands. But he tends to get a little frustrated when he's gone a few days without a sale, and I've worked to coach him and channel his confidence in the right direction to focus on remaining positive. He is learning to feel and understand the peaks and valleys in the business and that you must judge your performance over the long haul. And his production over time has been quite good. It's the responsibility of my managers and me to keep those who struggle with such emotions on an even keel and help turn droughts into learning experiences that can lead to an increase in self-belief. Lulls in our success or achievement aren't personal — they just come with the territory.

Then there's Ginger Lopez, the fixed operations manager for our Toyota store in Lawrence who has more than 30 years of experience working at auto dealerships. She has been with our operation for about the last eight. There aren't many women who run the fixed operations (service, parts, and body shop) at dealerships, but throughout her career she has been helping to prove that more gender equity is well-deserved. Her focus on customer service is emphasized within her team, and the department's follow-up with car owners on service reminders is outstanding.

She started her career as a secretary in a Chevrolet dealership in a small town near Joplin, Missouri, and worked her way up to be a department head. After the destructive tornado that hit Joplin in 2011, she wanted to move, and my previous service manager was getting ready to retire, so the timing for her to join us worked out well. When she eventually took over the department some of the employees hired by the old manager tried to make it tough on her. She knew how to deal with people who looked down on her, though. She knew her worth as a person and as a manager and would accept nothing but respect from those around her. Through contacts she had made at other dealerships, she replaced doubters and naysayers with people who wanted to work for her. Within her first year as manager, she almost doubled the gross profit of the service department.

She has such a great reputation both in our dealership and in the industry that she still attracts talent from outside our company. She's also a great role model for everyone in her department, and as a result we now have more young women joining our organization as technicians than ever before. Toyota has even appointed her to national committees on service. She exudes confidence in her abilities and believes in herself in a business that historically has been dominated by males. My only concern is what we'd do if she ever left us. She's a major asset to our organization.

Not long ago, she sent me a nice e-mail that meant a lot to me. She referred to me as a father figure to her in her career and wrote that she valued our relationship. Over the years she felt that she hadn't always been appreciated by some of the owners for whom she had worked and was not treated with the respect she deserved based on her production. I was gratified to know that my own respect for her gave her peace of mind to be able to focus on her work and her capacity to achieve. As managers, we should know how to appreciate people well. I learned this growing up, but many have to figure it out in other ways. It's true that not everyone will listen to us or work exactly the way we want, but they all deserve our respect and a chance to prove themselves. Many, like our fixed operations manager, will exceed our expectations again and again.

I've had a lot of relationships with people over the years, and I've discovered that people gravitate toward those who are confident and comfortable with themselves. If I'm comfortable in my own skin, I'm much more able to adapt to my surroundings and adjust to and understand other people and their perspectives. I'm not threatened by anything or anyone unfamiliar, and that's very appealing to others. By the same token, I don't need to feel offended when people don't gravitate toward me or want to be around me. Not everyone has to want me for their best friend or hang on every word I say. My ego can take it.

You can't let the noise and surroundings of naysayers change you as a person. Block that out and maintain your self-confidence and self-motivation. When I first started on the showroom floor, it seemed that about every 90 days I'd go into a slump. It seemed I wouldn't sell a car for a week, and then I'd get on a roll. It would have been easy to let my emotions and feelings of self-worth rise and fall with my successes and slumps, or to let my adherence to my values wane as slumps lingered. I had to learn how to remain my own self and look for ways to gain momentum from the contributions of a wide variety of people. You keep your eye on the achievers, and you can see their momentum building and help them capitalize on it.

Another tactic I recommend for maintaining your belief in yourself is to practice good health and fitness habits and to include a proper diet. Exercise doesn't have to be so intense that you're gasping for air or have aching muscles the rest of the day. A brisk 30-minute walk will do a lot to burn fat, reduce stress, and stimulate endorphins. Eating right, with lots of salads and fat-free foods, will prevent sluggishness and fatigue. I motivate myself to follow these practices, because once you head the other way it's hard to turn it around.

People often think of things like confidence as being purely mental issues and neglect the physical aspects, but our minds and bodies are connected, more connected than we like to admit sometimes. Good health breeds confidence.

• • • •

It's easy to say, "Be confident," but self-belief doesn't usually come naturally for most people. It must be developed like any other skill, and the decision to do so or not is yours. You can look for mentors and strong examples and form strong work habits. You can assess yourself and your experiences in ways that will help you learn and grow. You can find ways to stay grateful and surround yourself with people who support you. Or not. But I would encourage you to place your personal capital at risk, to take a chance not just on your career but on yourself. You have the power to affect the course of your life and career — if you have the courage.

Chapter 18
THE FINAL DASH

Principle #18: Leave a Legacy

"I want to leave the world a better
place for me having been here."
Dr. James Naismith

When **I** was inducted into the Lawrence Business Hall of Fame, I shared a favorite poem with the audience during my speech. Written by Linda Ellis in 1996, it's titled "The Dash," and deals with themes that I think about more and more as I get older — life, death, and our purpose while we're here. The first part of it goes like this:

> I read of a man who stood to speak
> at the funeral of a friend.
> He referred to the dates on the tombstone
> from the beginning . . . to the end.
>
> He noted that first came the date of birth
> and spoke the following date with tears,

but he said what mattered most of all
was the dash between those years.

For that dash represents all the time
that they spent alive on earth.
And now only those who loved them
know what that little line is worth.

The speaker in the poem then considers what really is of value and what people might change if they lived each day with more awareness that life is brief and we never really know how much of our own is left. We are encouraged to be kinder, more understanding, more loving, more respectful of those around us. After considering all this, the speaker ends with a question for the reader: At the end, "would you be proud of the things [others] say / about how you spent your dash?"

It's a question I ask myself as I consider my own legacy. It's a gravitas-filled idea because it's not just how you want to be remembered after you leave this world, it's also a window into what your life was about. A legacy should mirror what your standards and values are and serve as a guiding light and inspiration for friends and family members, in the next generation and beyond. It's not just what I may leave for my family, but what I have contributed to society during my time on earth.

If I had a biographer who would be there to sum everything up after I'm gone, I'd want to be remembered as someone who gave his best and worked hard, who raised a wonderful family and gave back to his community, and who above all treated people the right way. I would hope the writer would praise my parents and the strong value system they instilled in me. I would want them to interview my family, close friends, and business associates — people I was able to help and people who helped me. I hope it would show that my life has mattered in some small way.

Now, I have to tell you that I don't plan on dying. I can't even give a straight answer to people who ask when I'm retiring. I enjoy my current routine of living in Florida for six months of the year and living and working in Kansas City for the other six months, and I plan to keep on doing so. And Paula likes to chime in whenever she's around to say, "He thinks he's Peter Pan, and is going to live forever."

But forever is a long time. My old friend Larry Spitcaufsky figures I'll only make it to 100, and says he plans to be around to give the eulogy. I suppose I'll just have to continue to do what I'm doing for as long as I can do it and trust Larry to embellish at the end.

One morning several decades ago, when I was still in Decatur, I was listening to a radio interview with the late Joe Morgan, a Hall of Fame player for the Cincinnati Reds and later a broadcaster and baseball analyst for the national networks. He was a two-time National League Most Valuable Player for the Reds teams that won the World Series in 1975 and 1976. He is recognized by many baseball experts as the greatest all-around second baseman ever to play the game. He also was involved in several charitable organizations, including the Jackie Robinson Foundation. His was a full life that was well-lived both in and out of the public eye.

Joe was asked in the interview about all his accomplishments — not just in reference to his success on the diamond and in the broadcast booth, but also what he contributed to the communities where he lived. He responded that his father had put it into perspective for him as he was growing up. His dad had told him that if you're in a position to help people and you can make a difference for one person, then you can leave this world knowing you did the right thing and leave behind a legacy for helping people. That's what kept him going.

It made a whole lot of sense to me — that your ultimate level of success is defined by the people you have helped. And living by that credo is what keeps me going toward my own finish line. I know I'm not done in this world, and I have a desire to do more before I reach the end. The challenge is identifying that finish line — is it when I retire, is it when I die, is it when I sell the dealerships? I have no explanation. I've tried to figure that out and I've talked to a lot of people, particularly my family and spiritual advisors, trying to determine what it would be. Ultimately, I guess it means different things to different people, and I have yet to figure it out for myself.

• • • •

Of course, something is going to get me eventually, be it a long-term illness or something more sudden. I know those life insurance policies will pay off at some point. But I try not to dwell on that part. Instead, I get up every morning expecting to focus on life — maybe I'll have some fun, or go to work, or do something that positively affects someone else. Or maybe all three.

I've enjoyed many blessings over my 75 years. I was raised by great parents who loved me and led exemplary lives that inspired me. I hope I have done an equally good job of passing those traits down to my children and grandson. I also hope I have done a good enough job of sharing the many gifts I've received with others — whether they be material goods or just a word of encouragement.

As a young man I benefitted from exposure to some great mentors, who taught me not only the skills needed to run a successful business but also how to treat people so that you maximize their potential. It has been a source of great satisfaction to me to in turn provide similar mentorship to others. I am optimistic that part of my legacy will be that these capable and intelligent people I've been fortunate to influence and help on their way are out in the world also influencing others for good.

In terms of business, in my remaining years in the auto industry, I would like to buy some more deals. I was all set to do that with Volkswagen right before their deceptive practices scandal. I had just won the company's Diamond Pin award, which is given to dealers all over the world for operational excellence and is the highest honor for a VW franchise. Ali accompanied me to Germany for the reception, and I have to tell you it was a little surreal. For a Jewish boy born in the 1940s to receive an award given by a German company seemed like a moment out of a movie or a book — more fiction than reality. I wished more of the family could have been there.

At the time, I was considered one of VW's best dealers, and I was looking forward to capitalizing on my success before the emissions issue went public. After navigating through that crisis, two years of a pandemic, and a shortage of inventory, Volkswagen has put expansion on hold, as have the other manufacturers. At some point, however, they are going to look again at their footprint, and there are a couple of people with whom I may pool funds to buy dealerships in bigger markets rather than smaller towns. I still have the juices to do that. I don't just want to go to the clubhouse and just sit around playing bridge and drinking Scotch. There's more to me than what I've already done.

The industry has changed with people ordering their cars online and companies such as Tesla using a different distribution system, but the core business remains the same. The last three years have actually been record-breakers for us in fixed operations. I also don't see legislators allowing the franchise model to go away. Our dealership organization is a strong enough consortium that we can influence governing bodies to limit the sort of brokering that would harm the industry.

At the moment, it's true that more people are now holding onto their cars rather than trading them. Prices are high, product is scarce, but also the cars are built better and last longer with proper maintenance. But there are still a lot of people who want to walk into a dealership and do business face-to-face when it is time for a new vehicle. They may communicate with you online, but in the end they want to see the product and "kick the tires" before purchasing. I've seen a lot of changes, and there will probably be many more after I'm gone, but I'm optimistic about the future of the dealership structure.

As for my current company, if something happened to me tomorrow there is a succession plan. It's a sound business practice that some entrepreneurs put off doing until it is too late, but it is a necessity, and in my industry the manufacturers want them in place for the franchisees.

I would advise business owners to create similar plans for themselves sooner rather than later. I've known owners who died suddenly in accidents, leaving behind a family of three or four grown kids with some in the business and some not in the business. Then the spouses of the kids get involved and it's a mess. Everyone has their own idea of what's fair or right in the situation, and somehow those ideas are always different and often competing. My attorney came from a family of lawyers, including his father and brothers. They all advise their clients to deal only with the immediate family to make succession decisions while the owners are alive and able to state their desires clearly. You can take the guesswork out of asset allocation with a trust, or even a document as simple as a will, but in the case of a business I strongly encourage having a succession plan in place.

I also have a plan for leaving my family instructions about what will need to be done when I pass. It's important to direct your family on your wishes and who to go to for the practical details that can be hard to think about in moments of stress or loss (e.g., accountant, attorney, life insurance agent, etc.). This holds true even if you don't have a lot of assets. Cecil and I had our agreement on a yellow legal pad, so it can be as plain and simple as that, but it is preferable to use professional advisors to assist in navigating any legal hurdles. None of these things have been easy to think about or plan for, but I feel better knowing that the people I care about won't have to deal with extra hurdles in my absence just because I wanted to avoid some uncomfortable conversations now.

But what about now? What about before the plans are needed, before my family needs to read that letter? What else is left to accomplish? It's a question that weighs heavy on my mind. What I think about most is whether I'm wasting time, especially for the six months I'm not in town, when I'm away from the day-to-day operations of the dealerships. I know they're in good hands with my managers, so I need to find something else to keep me busy, engaged in the world and doing my best to leave a mark — for at least another 50 years. Okay, let's say 60. (Sorry, Larry — you'll just have to wait!)

As our business lives wane and our professional productivity decreases, we can't stay in neutral. We need to find something we love to focus on. I want to continue to support community and philanthropic organizations as much as I can. One way I have done that is to create a charitable fund from my Social Security checks. I deferred taking Social Security until I reached the age where it was required. It always felt like, if I took mine, somebody else who needed the checks more might not be able to get theirs, and in my mind and heart that didn't seem right. A couple of friends finally talked sense to me — if I didn't take my portion, the government sure as heck wasn't going to give it to someone else. So I decided to take that money and put it in a designated account for contributions. Then instead of running it through the company's philanthropic budget I give it away in support of causes I care about. For example, $1,000 per year is designated for CASA — the Court Appointed Special Advocates that work to support children suffering from abuse or neglect. It's not exactly passing out Social Security checks to people who need one, but it feels like the right thing to do.

With the extra time I have now I've also been investing in activities that keep me charged up and maybe make time go a bit slower. I'd like to take chef lessons, and with the establishment of our family wine company, I've really developed a love and appreciation of vintage stock and would like to be certified as a sommelier. The more I learn, the more I can accomplish with our brand, and perhaps make something big out of that.

Some years ago, I started taking piano lessons when my mom was in her late 90s, with the plan to play for her on her 100th birthday. My teacher was a classical pianist and was trying to teach me to play that type of music, which was a bit like trying to teach me how to fly by flapping my arms. I took an hour lesson with her every week for three or four years, and I was just getting to the point where I could play some things.

We had a 99th birthday celebration for Mom in December 2009. She was in pretty good shape mentally, although her body was starting to give out and she had a caregiver who provided 24-hour care. They had a piano at the retirement village where she lived, and we had family there, so I started playing something that sounded enough like music for about 10-15 minutes, and they brought Mom out in her wheelchair to listen. She died about nine months later, three months shy of her 100th birthday. I found out later from my sister that Mom thought it was her 100th when I played, so I satisfied my goal — in a way.

I read a story once about Nola Ochs, a woman who graduated from college in 2007 with a general studies degree with an emphasis in history from Fort Hays State University, about three hours from me down Interstate 70. Nola was 95 at the time. She graduated alongside her 21-year-old granddaughter. She had started college decades earlier and returned after she realized how close she was to earning her degree. She was later hired by Princess Cruises to be a guest lecturer on a Caribbean cruise, which had been her dream job for years. Not satisfied with all that, she earned her master's degree in 2010. At the time, she held the Guinness World Record for being the world's oldest college graduate. She's still the oldest person to earn a master's degree. Nola died in 2016 at the age of 105.

I think about Nola when I need a little inspiration to keep following my passions, to keep pursuing new ventures, to keep being curious, to keep learning.

• • • •

God gives us each talent, and it's up to us to take advantage of it. But you also need some help, and there is some luck involved on occasion. However you acquire your gifts, the important thing is to take what you are given and share it. I've attempted to do that through the things I have done philanthropically and by giving advice and support to young people. I hope I am thought of as someone who maybe brought some value to an individual I met in a chance encounter. People can sense what's in your heart, and if they know you care they'll feel better about themselves. That may put them on the road to success — I always hope it does — but it definitely makes you a success.

I've been asked what I want on my tombstone. My stock answer is I haven't thought that far in advance, because that means I'm planning for the end. And, succession plans aside, I'd rather not plan out the aftermath of my own death to that degree. It also feels like that's an assessment that should be made by those who loved you, but if I had to be pinned down, I'd hope it would read something like "I tried to do the right thing, and I was rewarded for it." But as it has been often said, we should carve our names on hearts instead of tombstones. I think that will be a far better epitaph.

THE DREAM

When I lived in Decatur, I was a member of the local chapter of the Rotary Club, a service organization that included a lot of area businesspeople, bankers, and some officers of not-for-profit organizations. One gentleman whose acquaintance I made through the club was Major Wert, who was in charge of the local Salvation Army. He was a good guy who had a big heart, and though I didn't know him that well I really admired him for what he did with his organization.

As I've mentioned, it has always been my practice not to screen my phone calls. If you want to get hold of me, you can get right in unless I'm on another call. Also, if you show up in person and I'm available I'll come down and meet you in the showroom. One day the receptionist at the dealership called and said that Major Wert was at her desk requesting to see me.

I assumed he was going to ask me about a sponsorship or other donation, to which I would usually respond by requesting a brochure or proposal that I would refer to my philanthropic committee. But when I went to greet him, he said he really needed to talk to me in my office.

I usually don't invite people into my office unless they have an appointment, mostly for the sake of time, but he looked like something was weighing heavily on his mind. I didn't know if it was a car problem or a personal issue, but I could tell it was something of importance to him. When we arrived at my office he asked if he could shut the door. He was starting to make me a little nervous, but I told him to go ahead.

What followed was one of the most unusual but impactful conversations I've ever had.

He sat down and said, "You know me. And you know I'm not crazy." At which we both chuckled.

"I had a dream last night," he continued. "In it, God told me to come and tell Miles Schnaer that he needed to start a men's club."

A little awestruck, I sat back in my chair and said, "Tell me more."

"I'm telling you that it was more than a dream. God actually told me your name and to go see you. We know each other from the Rotary Club, we see each other at the weekly luncheons and say hi, but we don't socialize or do other things together. I'm not asking for anything, I don't want anything, but I have to tell you this to get it off my conscience."

I asked him what God told him I should do next. He said he didn't know.

"I'm just telling you it was vivid, and that He said I needed to tell Miles Schnaer to start a men's club. I don't know if it is to benefit kids or some other charity. But I have to get this off my chest."

I've never forgotten that meeting. After I left Decatur, I never found out what became of Major Wert. I don't even know if he's still alive. But every time I've moved to a new city I've wondered if this is the location to initiate whatever it is God wants me to do. I did start a fishing club for kids in Lawrence that had some businessmen as sponsors and grew to a couple hundred members, but I keep thinking there's something more out there for me to do.

I've enjoyed many blessings and successes. I've traveled the world, met a lot of interesting, famous, and not-so-famous people, and taken the initiative to pay it forward whenever I can. But the memory of this one-time meeting with this unpretentious man has remained imbedded in my mind for more than three decades. I think it's part of the reason there's a hole in my heart that remains unfilled — I know I still have some unfinished business in my remaining years on this planet.

Chapter 19
RECAP AND APPLICATIONS

*"An army of principles will penetrate
where an army of soldiers cannot."*
Thomas Paine

I've been asked a number of times how I came up with the "Crown" name for my dealership brand. It's been very successful, and I think people wonder if it was inspired by British royalty, but it wasn't nearly that dramatic. In Decatur, we had Miles Chevrolet and Miles Nissan, and then I bought the old Toyota dealership. Cecil was my partner in those stores, and he and I were sitting around talking about the new acquisition, for which I wanted to continue to use the name "Miles." He thought that in a town the size of Decatur, if you have too many dealerships under the same name, people might think you're trying to be greedy and create a monopoly. And if they've had any negative experience at one shop, it might carry over to the new place under the umbrella of the same name. As usual his insights were spot-on — one of the reasons he enjoyed such great success in so many areas.

We started talking about possibilities for names over drinks — back then I drank Chivas Regal and he drank Crown Royal. We started throwing out potential names — "Paula Toyota," "Chivas Toyota" — all sorts of monikers — then I jokingly suggested to Cecil that in honor of him and his favorite libation we go with Crown. We laughed, but when I ran it by my marketing person later, he thought he could do a lot with it. We had our brand.

When I moved back to Kansas City and took over the Auto Plaza in Olathe, we renamed it Miles Auto Plaza. After the Auto Plaza was sold and I was looking at the dealerships in Lawrence, I had some concern the sale might lead people to think we might be buying the Lawrence shops to sell them later. Lawrence was only 40 miles away and people talk. We already had the Crown name and logos copyrighted in Decatur, and those stores had a great reputation if anyone wanted to check them out, so we went with Miles Schnaer's Crown Automotive, and it's been working well so far.

We got a little bit lucky with the brand name — some fly better than others — but I try not to rely on luck much. I've found that it's mostly hard work that makes a person "lucky." Success really is measured by the how well you manage your people and company culture, your internal processes, your product, and how you position or market it in the community. Have a command of those, and you'll find you won't need much luck.

There are two overriding ideals that have guided my life and my career. The first is broad in scope and encompasses the idea businesses and communities are necessarily interconnected. Satisfaction with just being a small part of a community and expecting to own a successful business won't work. The community needs your support, and in turn the businessowner needs the support of the community.

The second ideal is much more focused and personal and much more critical, as it is based in what's best for one's own family. For me this concept was underlined and made clear by Paula and my daughters when I was between Decatur and Kansas City, as I was contemplating adding more dealerships and perhaps moving again. "If you want to move, plan on going on your own." That's all I needed to hear to fix my game plan. I took care of those closest to me, which led me to establish the roots of my business nearby in Lawrence, and Crown Automotive has grown into one of the most successful dealerships in the Midwest. It had to be together; it had to happen with the support of the most important people in my life.

Family remains the overriding influence in my life, as it should be for all of us. I can write a pretty good speech, and I've given a lot over the years at employee and community functions. Speaking in public doesn't make me too nervous or cause much consternation at this point. (Paula does tease me that I need to have a beginning and an end, though, because people don't want to hear me babble on for hours.) But I'm like my dad in that when it comes to talking about family, I have a hard time holding it together. Underneath his tough exterior was a great, benevolent man with a lot of emotion that couldn't help but be seen in those moments. Similarly, when I begin to talk — or even just think — about my family, it's difficult to hold my feelings in check.

When Dad passed away in 1994, my mom and sisters felt that as the only son in the family — and a practiced public speaker — I should give the eulogy. The rabbi at the service talked to me ahead of time to see if I wanted to do it, and I told him I did, but I cautioned him that I might get too emotional. He said he expected that — he knew my dad was the same way. We made a plan. I left the printout of my eulogy on the podium, and I told the rabbi that when the time came for me to speak, he should look my way. If I shook my head, then he'd know I wouldn't be able to do it, and he should take over. He wanted me to do it, and I wanted to do it, but when the moment came I just couldn't. I shook my head, and without missing a beat he read my prepared text. It was the same when my mom died. I put my feelings down on paper, but Mandi had to read it for me. She cracked a few times but did a good job delivering it — much better than I could have done.

• • • •

I was asked years ago if I were going to start a university or college, what would it look like? My answer then hasn't changed: a college of common knowledge, a place where book learning and human understanding are both valued. Of course we need education to train doctors and lawyers, but to thrive in life we need to first teach ideas like tolerance and expression of thought. There is value in all people, regardless of gender, status, race, or political differences, and we should seek to listen to their voices just as much as we hope to have our own voices heard. And let us not to be afraid to stand up for our beliefs in a way to help others to think and make good positive decisions.

It would also be a place where entitlement would be minimized and coping skills would be maximized. All of us experience the sentiment of entitlement from time to time. It's human nature. But starting at the top of your field isn't a right. Real work is required, and that's going to involve learning to deal with stressful situations. Experts know that obtaining and maintaining good coping skills does take practice, but as we utilize them, they become easier over time. Most importantly, good coping skills make for good mental health.

Whether these are lessons learned in some institution of higher education or through life experience, they are necessary for those who want to become leaders in their organizations and in the community. These are the people who will be looked at to set the example. It is not hard to be a leader and a good person some of the time. It's very difficult to be a leader and a good person all of the time. Without that training in human understanding, it's impossible.

• • • •

My own gathering of life experiences has been quite a journey so far. Through it all, I've learned to rely on the 18 principles detailed in the preceding chapters. These did not magically come to mind on day one of my career. Rather, they have evolved with me through the decades, as each day I've attempted to learn something new.

And, of course, it all started with my upbringing by two loving parents. My mom was here long enough to witness some of my achievements, some of my life and business philosophy take shape, but my dad was gone before a lot of it happened. As stern as he could seem, I know he'd be proud. Paula turned my life around more than once, and thanks in large part to her, our two daughters turned out to be better people than I could have ever hoped. Then there's my grandson, Maddox, who continues to bring such joy to all our lives.

Maybe the greatest time of my life was when Maddox was about two. He and Mandi lived with us for about a year, as she was figuring out where the best place would be for her to establish residence for her job as a teacher. It was so much fun. He was so inquisitive and loved to explore the house. This was during my piano lesson days, and I had a keyboard in my home office. It didn't take him long to figure out how to turn it on, and he loved to come in and bang on it and sing songs. He's always called me "Gramps," and back then he would want to know everything I was doing and imitate me, even with something as simple as shaving.

We all went out to dinner one night and he and Paula were already seated when I walked in the room. He saw me from across the way and ran at me in a sprint, and then jumped in my arms. It felt so good that I thought my heart was going to jump out of my chest.

He's at the age now when I know I probably embarrass him a little, like the time I praised him on Facebook for his middle school graduation, but he's still my good buddy. He does very well in school — much better than his Gramps ever did. Maddox can probably accomplish more in one month of high school than I did in four years.

As he gets older and progresses in school we want to watch as many of his basketball games as we can. When we're not in Kansas we are able to stream his games at De Soto High online, and when we're in town we go in person. He's a sophomore who starts on the junior varsity team and gets to suit up for the varsity games. He's about 5-foot-9 and plays point guard, and his coaches at the high school and in Amateur Athletic Union leagues really like his efforts. He'll take a charge, direct the offense, and do whatever is needed to help the team win. Maddox loves basketball, and, short of making the NBA, he wants to be a sports agent. I don't think it's just the proud grandpa in me that says he has the traits that could make him very successful in that field.

I think sometimes about what I might tell him if Maddox were ever to come to me for advice as he's starting out on adulthood and a career of his own. I'd keep it brief: "Just be yourself." His self-esteem and self-confidence are good, and so is his self-discipline, thanks to his mother. He's grown up observing everything Mandi is involved with — from teaching school to personal training — and she and Paula have always done activities with him to make him feel as important as he truly is. (When he was five, I asked him who his best friend was, and while I was puffing out my chest expecting it to be me, he said without hesitation, "Grams.")

These are the people who have formed and continue to form me. It's been my privilege to be part of this family and the communities I've shared in. Their influence and my experiences with them, whether they be close relatives, mentors, peers, or teammates, have shaped the 18 principles that have provided a core structure for me and framed a lifetime of actions and decisions. The benefits to me have been overwhelming. I hope you'll use them to influence your life as well.

In one of my favorite stories, "The Cab Ride I'll Never Forget," author Kent Nerburn writes about one night during his former life as a cab driver on the night shift. He picks up an old woman who, he discovers, needs a ride from her home to a hospice facility where she would spend her final days. She has no family left, but she does have lots of memories, and along the way she asks that he take her through the city to visit the landmarks of her life one last time.

After two hours they finally arrive at the nursing home, where Nerburn refuses her offer of cab fare, gives her a hug, and then walks into the light of dawn as the door closes behind him: "It was the sound of the closing of a life."

He writes that he drove aimlessly for the remainder of his shift, reflecting on his experience and the woman. "We are conditioned to think that our lives revolve around great moments," he writes. "But great moments often catch us unaware — beautifully wrapped in what others may consider a small one."

It's my hope for myself as much as for you that we all become more aware of those great, small moments before the closing of our own lives. Weekends spent barrel racing with my best friend, getting set up on a date by a fraternity brother, taking a chance on a new hire who becomes a trusted partner, pretending to shave with my grandson, playing the piano for my mother — this is the stuff our lives are made of, the stuff my life is made of. Even as we strive to have success in our careers and pursuits, let us never lose sight of who and what it is really for.

ACKNOWLEDGEMENTS

There have been many who have inspired me to undertake this project, and to share the lessons of life, both professionally and personally. Each day I lean on my faith in God and my upbringing by two loving parents who taught me to do the right thing and pass it on. I was also influenced by my sisters, Bonnie and Madeline, along with their families.

Paula has encouraged me along the way, and so have our two daughters, Mandi and Ali, and our grandson, Maddox. The life lessons taught by other family members have been included in this work as well, including Paula's parents, Jim and Jean Beebe, and sister, Sandi Norton, and my aunt Mary Greenstein, who was like a second mom to me.

None of this would have ever happened without the opportunities afforded me by Cecil and Ruby Van Tuyl and their family. He showed me how hard work translates into success, which I have stated several times in this book. I am grateful to my other mentors in the early days at Van Chevrolet, too — Jerry Dahmer, Frank Stinson, Ron Huber. Mike Stewart, another Van alumnus, continues to be an invaluable resource to me as a business owner. My appreciation also goes out to Leon Morse, who gave me my first chance, and to my lifelong "Comanchero" friend, Larry Spitcaufsy, who recommended I get into the car business in the first place.

Thanks to Kendall Gammon, Bill Self, Bob Carter, Sharon Spratt, Larry Van Tuyl, Dr. Steve Scott, Scott Bell, Don McNeely, Sheahon Zenger, and Kurt Falkenstien. Your words and wisdom have assured me on this project, as well as over many years.

I am thankful to Brenda Roberts, my office manager and right-hand person who has kept me organized since I bought the Lawrence dealerships in 1994. Along with her, my general managers, Randy Habiger and Jake Sacks, and my fixed operations manager, Ginger Lopez, continue to run my companies so well that I'm able to pursue personal interests like this one while the business remains strong. I greatly appreciate their contributions to this story, along with the other members of my Lawrence team.

Dan Duryee, the winemaker at Lady Hill, also helps me find inspiration to continue to try new things. His knowledge of his industry has resulted in a new passion for me to pursue. And other friends and former associates who have pushed me to put my principles in writing for some time deserve a special thanks as well: Rabbi Zalman Teichtel, John Hampton, Pat Dawson, Pat Bello, Tony Winslow, Steve Horve, Gordie Short, Steve Brace, Tom McNamara, Brian Hanni, Pat Henderson, and Jim Johnson. I especially want to acknowledge others who provided knowledge, friendship, and inspiration that culminated in these pages, but are no longer here to see it come to fruition: Dale Backs, Dick Nagy, Dennis Wilson, Bob Brilley, Lloyd Stewart, and Max Falkenstien.

And finally, thanks to those who worked to bring this project to life: my publisher and friend at Ascend Books, Bob Snodgrass, for providing the vision; my co-author, Mark Fitzpatrick, for translating my thoughts into meaningful prose; and my editor, Courtney Brown, whose research and mastery of the language made it all better.

There are other friends and influencers too numerous to mention. Cecil once said that when we die we're lucky to have a handful of friends at our bedside. I feel like I'll have standing room only. I have truly been blessed.

ABOUT THE AUTHORS

Miles Schnaer is the owner of the Crown Organization, a multi-brand auto dealership based in Lawrence, Kansas. In his 50-year career in automotive sales covering three states, he has won numerous industry awards and has been named *Time* magazine's Dealer of the Year for his state in both Illinois and Kansas. In 2017, Schnaer was inducted into the Lawrence Business Hall of Fame. A native of Kansas City, Missouri, he graduated from Pittsburg State University, where he met his future wife, Paula. The university's Alumni Association named him a recipient of its highest honor, the Meritorious Achievement Award in 2015. In 2014, his entrepreneurial skills led him to the Willamette Valley in Oregon, where he founded Schnaer Family Wines. Since that time, the winery has produced four award-winning vintages. An avid golfer and sports fan, he now divides his time between Fort Myers, Florida, and Lawrence. He is the proud father to Ali and Mandi, as well as grandfather to Maddox.

Mark Fitzpatrick has served as a writer and editor for a variety of publications. He began his career in the sports information departments of Stanford University and the University of Missouri, where he won several national awards for his media guides. He has also been a contributing writer to *Strong of Heart*, a periodical published by the Notre Dame Athletics Department. A sports public address announcer on every level from junior high to the professional ranks, he has been the voice of the Big 12 and Big Eight Basketball Tournaments since 1982. In 2020, he retired from a 36-year banking career in Kansas City, Missouri, where he resides with his wife, Nancy. The couple has four children and three grandchildren.